Saxon Activity Guide
for
Middle Grade Series

Appropriate for use with Math 54 and above

Stephen Hake

SAXON PUBLISHERS, INC.

Saxon Activity Guide for Middle Grade Series

Copyright © 1994 by Saxon Publishers, Inc.

Printed in the United States of America

ISBN: 1-56577-028-5

Production Supervisor: David Pond

Production Coordinator: Joan Coleman

Graphic Artist: John Chitwood

Seventh printing, July 2003

Reaching us via the Internet

WWW: www.saxonpublishers.com

E-mail: info@saxonpublishers.com

Saxon Publishers, Inc.
2450 John Saxon Blvd.
Norman, OK 73071

PREFACE

This teacher's *Activity Guide* provides a hands-on, manipulative-based series of fifty activities gathered into six thematic units that integrate several mathematical strands. Designed to accompany the Saxon middle-grades texts, these activities may also be used to provide valuable augmentation to other basal mathematics programs. Teachers are encouraged to use this guide to provide classroom activities for their students throughout the year.

Most of the activities are composed of two parts: first, a review of learning from previous activities, then the new activity. The emphasis during review is upon mental math facility and problem solving. An almanac activity is also included in the review section. We suggest that an almanac activity begin class every day. The routine for the daily almanac activity is provided in the course of the first eight activities.

The review exercises should be presented orally. For most of the mental math review exercises, a choral response is appropriate and is recommended. If an individual response is indicated, provide opportunity for all students to consider how they would respond before selecting a child. Teachers should feel free to expand upon the mental math exercises provided in each activity.

The problem-solving portion of the review section often calls for students to make a list, draw a sketch, or act out an activity. Many problems can be solved in a variety of ways. Teachers are encouraged to ask students to describe various strategies used to solve the problems posed.

Following the review section is the new activity. Most of the activities in this guide are brief and need not consume an entire math period. The majority should be able to be completed within 15 to 20 minutes. Expect activities that involve cutting paper or taking measurements to take a larger portion of class time.

We suggest that the unit "Almanac" be completed as early in the year as possible and that an almanac activity be used to start each day for the balance of the year. The routine for the almanac review is presented in Activities 5–8. The activities from subsequent units may be presented as time and opportunity allow. Many of the activities from the *Activity Guide* provide active support to the basal math program. In Unit 2, for example, students are asked to assemble a "money pouch" with the decimal value bills and coins. The manipulatives used in this unit may also serve to improve student understanding of related topics presented in textbooks.

The activities in this guide may also be used to make connections to other subject areas. Geography, home economics, meteorology, art, and writing are examples of other subject areas addressed in these math activities. Teachers are encouraged to link other subject areas to mathematics as opportunities arise.

The activity sheets needed for the activities are contained in the appendix as masters. Manipulative materials needed for each activity are listed prior to the activity and are generally available in any classroom. Previewing upcoming activities will alert the teacher to materials that may need to be brought into the classroom.

A variety of typefaces are used in this *Activity Guide* as visual cues. Text in standard type provides general information or suggestions to the teacher. ***Bold italics*** are used to indicate suggested teacher questions or comments to be directed to the class. *Normal italics* indicate possible student responses. Text in normal italics between horizontal lines highlight key ideas to be emphasized during the activity.

TABLE OF CONTENTS

Table of Contents

LIST OF MASTERS

UNIT 1   ALMANAC

"Almanac" is a data collection and display unit. Some of the activities in this unit are designed to be continued throughout the school year. During this unit students will gather and graph data gathered from the newspaper or from direct measurement about daily weather conditions and times of sunrise and sunset. Students will also practice reading time from a clock and dates from a calendar.

A bulletin board is an important component of this unit. A suggested arrangement of the bulletin board is illustrated below. The graphs along the bottom of the bulletin board are developed daily and may remain in place for the entire school year. Copies of Masters 1 and 2 may be used to make the two graphs.

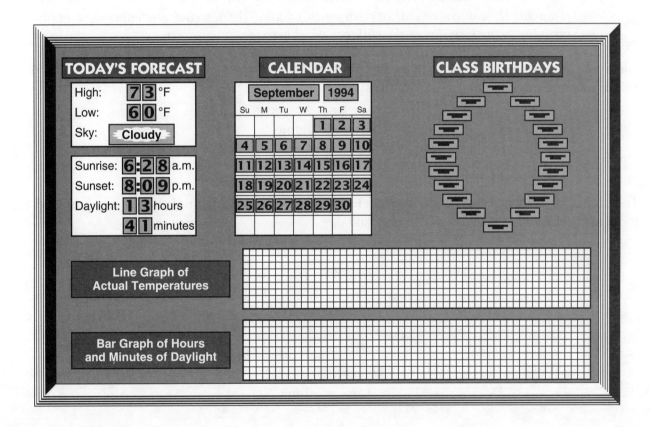

1

Activity 1   **Birthday Circle**

Materials Needed

- One 2" × 6" strip of light colored construction paper for each student

- Crayons or markers for students to write names and birthdays on the strips

Problem-Solving Activity

The task is for each student in the room to find the person in the room whose birthday is closest to his or her own birthday. (The activity also serves as an early "mixer" for the children.) The activity is structured to quickly reduce each student's search to two students by first having the students physically arrange themselves in order of their birthdays. (Note: Students should ignore year of birth for this activity.) Then each student compares his or her birthday to the birthday of the children on either side.

Distribute a construction paper strip to each student. Have students print their names and the month and day (not year) of their birthdays on the strips.

> **Student's name**
> **Month/Day**

Then have the students stand with their labeled strips and arrange themselves in a circle around the room in order of their birth dates by month and day.

Dec. Jan. Feb.

Nov.   Mar.

Oct.   Apr.

Sept.   May

Aug. July June

Provide some initial guidance by pointing out areas of the room where students with birthdays in certain months should stand. Students should be able to arrange themselves in order within a few minutes.

When the students are arranged in order, have them find which of the two persons next to them has a birthday closest to their own. This may also take a few minutes. Once the determination is made, students will need to remember that person's name and birth date.

Before students return to their seats, you may want to collect the strips in order. Later the strips may be mounted in a circular arrangement for a bulletin board display. Some possible bulletin board arrangements are illustrated at the end of this activity.

Once students have returned to their seats, have them write the name and birthday of the person in the class whose birthday is closest to their own. This information will be needed for a brief follow-up writing activity.

Discussion: Ask volunteers to describe how they decided which student's birthday was closest to their own. (A strategy for counting days is presented in Activity 3.) *"Can a person born in another month have a birthday closer to yours than a person born in the same month as you were?"*

Writing follow-up: Have each student write a brief paragraph stating his/her name and birth date, the name and birth date of the student in the class whose birthday is closest to his/her own, and how many days apart their birthdays are.

Example: "My name is _____. My birthday is _____. The person in the class whose birthday is closest to mine is _____. His/her birthday is _____. My birthday is _____ days before/after _____'s birthday."

Bulletin board: Displaying student birthdays in a circular arrangement emphasizes the cyclical nature of our calendar. A clockwise order is recommended. Allow enough bulletin board space for a 36-inch diameter circle.

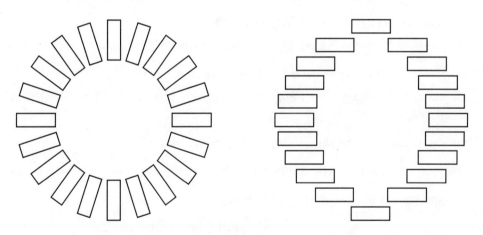

Activity 2

Months of the Year •
Counting by 4's, 7's, and 12's

The following questions and answers are offered to guide the class through a review of the months of the year:

"What is a year?"

A year is the number of days it takes the earth to travel around the sun.

"How many days does that journey take?"

The earth completes a trip around the sun in about $365\frac{1}{4}$ days.

"How many days are in a year?"

There are 365 days in a common year and 366 days in a leap year.

"Which years are leap years?"

Years that are multiples of four are leap years. By looking at the last two digits of the year, we can tell if the year is a multiple of four. Leap years end with '04, '08, '12, '16, '20, and so on.

"What special events occur in leap years?"

In modern history we elect U.S. presidents and hold summer Olympic games in leap years.

"To which month is the extra day added in leap years?"

We add the extra day to February. February has 28 days in common years and 29 days in leap years.

"How many days are in the other months of the year?"

Here are two ways to remember the number of days in the twelve months of the year:

• One way is to remember this jingle:

Thirty days hath September,
April, June, and November.

These four months have 30 days, February has 28 or 29 days, and all the rest of the months have 31 days.

• A second way to recall the number of days in a month is to use the knuckles on your fist. As you point to the first knuckle say "January." As you point between the first and second knuckles say "February." As you point to the second knuckle say "March." Continue up and down the knuckles to the fourth knuckle (July) and then come back to the first knuckle (August). Continue to December. The months on the knuckles have 31 days. The months between the knuckles have 30 days, except for February, which has 28 or 29 days.

January
February
March
April

"To use the knuckle method we need to know the months of the year in order. Let's say the months of the year in order as we practice the knuckle method."

Say the months in order. Practice two or three times.

"Now I will name some months and you tell me how many days are in these months."

Allow time for students to think of answers. Select voluntary responses. Inquire which method was used and why.

"What chart or table do we use to keep track of the days of the week and the days of the month?"

We use a calendar.

"This calendar is for which month?"

Refer to the calendar in the room.

"How many columns are in a calendar? Why?"

There are seven columns, one for each day of the week.

"How many rows are there? What does each row stand for?"

Most calendars are drawn with five rows. Each full row shows one full week.

"Did you know that a calendar can help you count by sevens?"

Find 7 on the calendar.

"What number is below the 7? What number is below 14? What number is below 21? Let's practice counting by sevens together."

7, 14, 21, 28, 35, 42, 49, 56, 63, 70, 77, 84 (These may be posted.)

"How many days are in one week? Two weeks? Three weeks? Four weeks? Five weeks? Ten weeks?"

Daily practice will prepare students for these multiplication facts.

"Leap years occur every four years. Let's practice counting by fours."

4, 8, 12, 16, 20, 24, 28, 32, 36, 40, 44, 48 (These may be posted.)

"There are 12 months in a year. Let's practice counting by twelves."

12, 24, 36, 48, 60, 72, 84 (These may be posted.)

"How many months are in one year? Two years? Three years? Four years? Ten years?"

Note: Counting by 7's, 4's, and 12's will be practiced for many activities. Posting these sequences for a couple of weeks will assist the students during the first few review sessions.

Activity 3   **Counting the Days Between Birthdays**

Review

- Count by 7's from 7 through 84.
- How many days are in one week? Two weeks? Three weeks? Ten weeks?
- Name the leap years from '00 through '96.
- How many months are in one year? Two years? Three years? Ten years?
- Name the months of the year using the knuckle method.
- Count by 10's from 10 to 100, from 5 to 95, and from 3 to 93.

Problem-Solving Activity: Counting Strategy

Students will practice two strategies for counting days in this activity.

Determine the student in the class whose birthday is next (or today) and record that student's name and birthday on the board.

From the birthday circle, have students determine whose birthday follows and whose birthday precedes the selected student's birthday. Record their names and birthdays on the board as well.

Have students determine the number of days between the selected student's birthday and the birthdays of the two other students. Have class members offer their answers and counting strategies.

A common mistake made by children when counting days is to begin by counting the selected day. We count from the selected day, but we do not count that day. (Tomorrow is one day away, not two.) Of course, subtraction can be used. However, one purpose of the lesson is to begin developing counting strategies, including counting elapsed time. Suggest these two strategies for counting days:

First strategy: Count weeks, then days on a calendar. When counting on a calendar between days that are more than one week apart, we can quickly count down the calendar by sevens and then sideways by ones. From the 8th to the 25th is two weeks and three days, which is 17 days.

		1	2	3	4	5
6	7	⑧	9	10	11	12
13	14	15	16	17	18	19
20	21	22	23	24	㉕	26
27	28	29	30	31		

Second strategy: When counting between days with or without a calendar, counting by tens and then by ones may speed the count. From the 3rd to the 25th we could count "13, 23, 24, 25." We counted by tens from 3 to 13 to 23 and by ones from 23 to 24 to 25 for a total of 22 days.

We can use this strategy for counting between days in adjacent months. Counting from April 15 to May 8, we count ten days to April 25, ten more to May 5, and then three more days to May 8, for a total of 23 days. Note that from May 15 to June 8 is 24 days because we need to add a day to our count for May 31st.

Activity 4   Diagrams for Counting Months

Review

- Count by 2's from 2 to 32.

- Count by 10's from 4 to 94, from 16 to 106, and from 1 to 101.

- Starting at the seventh on the calendar, count by 7's to 28 and then on to 84.

- How many days are in two weeks? Three weeks? Four weeks? Ten weeks? Eleven weeks? Twelve weeks?

- How many days are in a common year? In a leap year?

- Review the "Thirty days …" jingle.

counting strategies

- How many days are there from the 3rd of September to the 24th of September? (Count by 7's down the calendar.)   *21 days*

- How many days are there from September 15 to October 10? From October 15 to November 10?   *25 days; 26 days*

- Select 3 consecutive birthdays from the class and have students determine the number of days between the birthdays and which birthdays are closest together.

Problem-Solving Activity

Drawing a diagram and making a list are two problem-solving strategies which may be employed in this lesson to solve the problems posed. Ask students to make a list or diagram to help answer these questions.

First problem: *"Which month is halfway between February and June?"* Here are two diagrams students may use:

April is two months after February and two months before June. Encourage students to share how they arrived at their answer.

Second problem: *"Which month is halfway between May and September?"*   *July is two months after May and two months before September.*

Note: In preparation for Activity 5, ask students to bring the weather report page from a local newspaper. Alternatively, prepare sufficient copies of a weather report page to distribute one report per two students.

Kaitlyn → Dublin, Ireland
Emily →

Activity 5   **Weather Report and Forecast •**
Temperature Graph

Review

- How many days are in a common year? In a leap year?

- Name the months of the year in order across knuckles.

- Count by 2's from 2 to 32.

- Count leap years from '00 to '96.

- Review counting by 7's and the number of days in various numbers of weeks.

- Review counting by 12's and the number of months in various numbers of years.

problem solving

- How many days are there from June 22 to July 12?   *20 days*

- Which month is halfway between March and July?   *May*

Materials Needed

- Weather report from local newspaper with yesterday's high and low temperatures and today's predicted high and low temperatures (enough for pairs of students in the class)

- Prepared grid for line graph of daily highs and lows on bulletin board (Master 1)

Note: Master 1 is pre-marked for Fahrenheit temperatures from –30°F to 120°F. You may choose to re-mark for a different range of temperatures or for degrees Celsius.

Introduction

A newspaper weather report usually describes what the weather was like yesterday and predicts what the weather will be like today and in the near future.

"What is another word for a weather prediction?"

A weather prediction is a forecast.

"What is the name for a person who studies the weather?"

A person who studies the weather is a meteorologist. A newspaper weather report describes local weather and may describe weather in other parts of the country and other parts of the world as well. Meteorologists all over the world report the weather conditions from large cities, from small towns, from tiny islands, and even from ships at sea.

"What are some weather conditions a meteorologist may describe?"

Weather conditions measured and described by meteorologists include temperature, precipitation (rainfall, snowfall, etc.), wind direction and wind speed, relative humidity, and atmospheric pressure.

Ask students to find on the weather report yesterday's (preceding day's) high and low temperatures for your local area. Elicit responses from students. See that all students are able to locate the information. Record the high and low temperatures for all to see.

Graphing Activity

Keep a **graph** of the daily high and low temperatures on the bulletin board. (Each student may also keep a personal graph in a notebook, if desired.) Draw attention to the graph's vertical temperature scale and horizontal date scale.

You may want to ask a student to place a dot on the graph for yesterday's high temperature and another dot for yesterday's low temperature. Rotating this task through the class will give each student several opportunities to act in this role throughout the year.

Point out that the difference between the high and low temperatures is the **range** of temperature. Have students practice the mental math strategy of counting forward from the low temperature to the high temperature to mentally calculate yesterday's temperature range.

Ask students to locate on the weather report the forecasted high and low temperatures for today. Have a student read the forecast while you or a selected student record the predicted high and low temperatures on the "Forecast" portion of the bulletin board. Also record the "Sky" forecast (e.g., clear, cloudy, chance of rain, etc.).

Ask whether the forecast conditions are *certain* to develop or *likely* to develop.

Announce that tomorrow (or the next school day) the class will decide the accuracy of the forecast.

Activity 6   **Reading a Thermometer**

Review

- How many days are in a common year? In a leap year?

- Count by 2's from 0 to 32.

- Repeat together the "Thirty days …" jingle.

- Count leap years from '00 to '96.

- Use a calendar to count the number of weeks and days from the 9th to the 25th. How many days is that?   *2 weeks, 2 days; 16 days*

- Use a calendar to begin counting by 7's from 7 to 84.

- Count the number of months in one, two, three, four, and five years.

problem solving

- How many days are there from September 12 to October 5? From October 12 to November 5?   *23 days; 24 days*

- Which month is halfway between August and December?   *October*

Materials Needed

- Today's weather report from a newspaper as well as reports from the days since Activity 4 (To continue the activity through the year, the weather reports will be needed on a daily basis for every day of the school year, including weekends and holidays.)

- Celsius and Fahrenheit scale thermometers: at least one of each in the classroom and one of each outside the room

Thermometer Activity

Announce and post yesterday's (Activity 5) high and low temperatures. Ask students to compare the actual temperatures to the forecasted temperatures and to evaluate the accuracy of the forecast.

Ask a student to make dots on the temperature graph of the bulletin board to show the high and low temperatures for yesterday's date. Determine whether yesterday's temperatures were higher or lower than the previous day's temperatures. Calculate yesterday's temperature range.

Ask a student to post the forecast for today on the bulletin board.

"How does today's predicted weather compare to yesterday's weather? (Warmer? Cooler? Wetter? Drier?)"

"What instrument is used to measure temperature?"

The word thermometer is made up of two Greek words meaning "heat" and "measure."

"How does a thermometer work?"

A thermometer is usually a tube that contains a liquid, usually mercury or colored alcohol. As heat increases, the molecules in the liquid bump into each other with more force, causing the liquid to expand and move up the tube. As heat decreases, the liquid moves down the tube.

"How is a thermometer read?"

Next to the tube of liquid on a thermometer is a scale, or a series of marks. Usually there is a mark for every two degrees. To find the temperature, we locate the point on the scale that is even with the top of the liquid in the tube. There are two different scales commonly used to measure temperature: the Fahrenheit scale and the Celsius scale. The Fahrenheit scale is often marked with a capital "F." This scale is customarily used in the United States to describe the weather or temperatures for cooking. The Celsius scale, abbreviated with a capital "C," is commonly used in the rest of the world. The temperature in a classroom might be 68°F, which is 20°C.

"At what temperatures does water freeze and boil?"

Water freezes, that is, turns to ice, at 32°F, which is 0°C. Water boils, that is, turns to steam, at 212°F, which is 100°C.

Have students read the temperature from a thermometer inside the room and a thermometer outside the room. Students should avoid handling the thermometer because the heat from their hands may affect the temperature of the thermometer.

Activity 7   **Temperature Line Graph •**
                                               Sunrise and Sunset

Review

- At what temperatures does water freeze and boil on the Fahrenheit and Celsius scales?

- Repeat the months of the year in order.

- How many weeks and days are there from the 6th to the 31st? Altogether, how many days is that?   *3 weeks, 4 days; 25 days*

- Count leap years from '00 to '96.

- Starting with a calendar, count by 7's from 7 to 84.

- Count the number of months in one through seven years (12's).

problem solving

- How many days are there from November 11 to December 25? From December 11 to January 25?   *44 days; 45 days*

- What month is halfway between January and September?   *May*

Materials Needed

- Weather report from local newspaper that includes time of sunrise and sunset

Activity

Each day announce and post the previous day's high and low temperatures and ask students to compare actual temperatures to forecasted temperatures.

Select a student to graph the posted high and low temperatures by marking a dot for both temperatures at the correct date. The distance between the dots represents the range of temperature. Have students mentally calculate the range.

Temperature Line Graph

Ask a student to draw line segments connecting in order by date the dots graphed for the high temperatures. A second set of segments should also be drawn connecting the dots for the low temperatures.

Pose these questions to the class:

"What do the dots on the temperature graph show?"

The dots show the high and low temperatures for the day.

"What do the line segments between the dots mean?"

The line segments do not show the temperature. The line segments between the dots help us to compare temperatures. If the segments slope upward from left to right, this shows that the temperature from day to day is rising, or getting warmer.

"What would the line segments show if they sloped downward?"

> *If the segments slope downward from left to right, this shows that day-to-day temperatures are falling, or getting cooler.*

"If the day-to-day temperatures were about the same, what would the line segments on the graph look like?"

> *If the temperatures are not changing, the line segments will not slope upward or downward. The segments will be "level" or horizontal.*

Sunrise and Sunset

A weather forecast often includes the local time of sunrise and sunset. Announce and post today's time of sunrise and sunset.

Ask students to consider the comparative reliability of the temperature forecast and the "predicted" time of sunrise and sunset.

Clarify that cloud cover, buildings, or other obstacles may block our view of the sun so that we might not be able to see the sun at the time stated. The times for sunrise and sunset assume an unobstructed path for the sun's light to our location.

Calculating Hours and Minutes of Daylight

- Each day have students calculate the number of hours and minutes from sunrise to sunset and record the number on the section of the bulletin board for "Sunrise/Sunset/Daylight." This effortful calculation incorporates several computational strategies which are empowering when practiced daily.

Ask the class how many hours there are from sunrise to sunset. Some students may respond that there are 12 hours. In September there are close to 12 hours of daylight. Have students use that information and the posted times for sunrise and sunset to calculate how many hours and minutes of daylight there are today. Have students who are able to perform the calculation explain the mental or paper-and-pencil strategies they employed. Post the number of hours and minutes of daylight on the bulletin board.

Example:	**Sunrise:**	6:10 a.m.
	Sunset:	5:56 p.m.
	Daylight:	11 hours
		46 minutes

Activity 8   **Daylight Bar Graph**

Review

- Review the number of days in common years and leap years.

- Repeat the "Thirty days …" jingle.

- Which month is four months after November?   *March*

- How many days are in _____ weeks? (Ask several questions.)

- How many months are in _____ years? (Ask several questions.)

- How many weeks and days are there from the 7th to the 24th? Altogether, how many days is that?   *2 weeks, 3 days; 17 days*

problem solving

- How many days are there from April 3 to May 11? From May 3 to June 11?   *38 days; 39 days*

- What month is halfway between November and March?   *January*

Materials Needed

- Sunrise and sunset times for the day of the week which is the same day of the week as September 22

- Prepared grid for the bar graph for the number of hours and minutes of daylight (Master 2)

Activity

In this activity the class will begin a bar graph of the number of hours and minutes of daylight. This graph should be completed weekly for the same day each week. Select the day to graph that is the same day of the week as September 22. (This may turn out to be a weekend day, which could be graphed on Monday.) Using the September 22 day of the week will allow for the graphing of the approximate autumn and spring equinox and the shortest day of the year in December. The graph can aid the explanation of the astronomical events that mark the first day of fall, winter, spring, and summer. Students may also keep a personal graph, if desired.

Announce and post the previous day's weather conditions and compare with the forecast. Select a student to graph the temperatures.

Announce and post today's forecast. Ask how today's forecast compares with the previous day's weather conditions (i.e., warmer, cooler, wetter, drier, etc.).

Announce and post today's sunrise and sunset times. Have students calculate the number of hours and minutes of daylight and select successful students to explain their strategies.

Ask students to consider the amount of time each day that the sun cannot be seen in the sky.

"How many hours are in a day?"

>   *A day is 24 hours.*

"If it is daylight for 12 hours, then how many hours of a day is it not daylight?"

>   *If there are 12 hours when the sun can be seen, then there are 12 hours when the sun cannot be seen, because the total must be 24 hours. Distinguish between "daylight," when the sun is above the horizon, and "twilight" (dusk or pre-dawn, "dawn's early light"), when the sun is below the horizon.*

"If there are 12 hours and 30 minutes of daylight in a day, then how many hours and minutes can the sun not be seen?"

>   *If the sun can be seen for 30 minutes more than 12 hours, then it cannot be seen for 30 minutes less than 12 hours, which is 11 hours and 30 minutes.*

"How many hours and minutes today can the sun not be seen?"

Daylight Bar Graph

Select a day of the week which is the same day of the week as September 22. Announce the sunrise and sunset times for that day and have students calculate the number of hours and minutes of daylight. Begin a bar graph on the bulletin board that displays the hours and minutes of daylight. A bar should be drawn once a week for the same day of the week throughout the year. Thus, students calculate the hours and minutes of daylight each day and graph it once each week.

UNIT 2   DOLLARS AND SENSE

"Dollars and Sense" is a manipulative-based unit that uses currency to strengthen place value concepts and computational understanding. In this unit students assemble a money kit composed of pennies, dimes, 1-dollar, 10-dollar, and 100-dollar bills. The bills can be copied from Masters 3, 4, and 5. Pennies may be provided by the teacher or students. Using plastic coins or other substitute for dimes is recommended. Each student or pair of students will require 20 examples of each denomination. A "zip-locking" bag might be used to store the coins and bills. Students will use money from the kit to demonstrate place value and addition, subtraction, and multiplication concepts.

Activity 9   Money Pouch • Expanded Form

Review

almanac

- Graph the high and low temperatures and evaluate the forecast daily.

- Calculate the hours and minutes of daylight daily and graph weekly.

mental math

- Count up and down by 2's between 0 and 32.

- Repeat the months in order across knuckles.

- Count leap years from '00 through '96.

- Count by 7's and by 12's to 84.

Announce that we are starting an activity unit about money. Begin by practicing counting by dimes, nickels, and quarters:

- Count from 10¢ to a dollar (100¢) and backward from a dollar to 10¢.

- Count from 5¢ to a dollar and backward from a dollar to 5¢.

- Count from 25¢ to two dollars and backward from two dollars to 25¢.

problem solving

- How many days are there from January 1 to February 2?   *32*

- How many days are there from February 1 to March 2 in a leap year?   *30*

- What month is halfway between October and February?   *December*

Materials Needed

• Play money for $1, $10, and $100 bills (20 of each denomination for each student or pair of students). Masters 3, 4, and 5 may be copied to make bills for this unit.

• Envelopes or other pouches for students to store their play money

Activity

Money pouch: Distribute play money and storage materials. If students will be working individually, they each will need 20 copies of each denomination of bill. If students will be working in pairs, 20 copies of each bill per pair of students is sufficient. The play money should be stored by students in an organized and accessible manner. If students are cutting apart copies of Masters 3, 4, and 5, allow most of the activity time for this purpose.

Expanded form: Students may note that three commonly circulated bills are missing from their collection. The $5, $20, and $50 bills are convenient in reducing the number of bills we need to buy and sell products and services. However, the purpose of these activities is to improve each student's sense of place value. For this purpose we will use only $1, $10, and $100 bills.

Ask students to place $12 on their desks. Observe students to see if any children use 12 ones to display the sum. Explain that there are two ways to show $12 using their bills:

> 1 ten + 2 ones   or   12 ones

Now ask students to use the *fewest bills necessary* to show $123.

> 1 hundred + 2 tens + 3 ones

We can write $123 in **expanded form** as

> 1 hundred + 2 tens + 3 ones
>
> $100 + $20 + $3

Next ask students to show $203.

> 2 hundreds + no tens + 3 ones
>
> $200 + $3

Then ask students to show $350.

> 3 hundreds + 5 tens + no ones
>
> $300 + $50

As time allows, ask students to use their bills to show other amounts of money. Have students write each amount displayed in expanded form.

Activity 10   **Using Money to Add**

Review

almanac

- Perform daily activities.

mental math

- What month is twelve months after September?
- Count by 7's. Count by 12's.
- Count up and down by 2's between 0 and 32.
- At what temperatures does water freeze and boil on the Fahrenheit scale?
- At what temperatures does water freeze and boil on the Celsius scale?
- Nickels: Count up and down between 5¢ and one dollar.
- Dimes: Count up and down between 10¢ and two dollars.
- Quarters: Count up and down between 25¢ and three dollars.

problem solving

- How many days are there from January 15 to February 5?   *21*
- How many days are there from February 15 to March 5 in a common year?   *18*
- What month is halfway between September and May?   *January*

Materials Needed

- Play money for $1, $10, and $100 bills

Activity

Students will combine amounts of money to illustrate addition. Then students will be asked to visualize the process and perform the calculation mentally. An important skill in mental math is calculation from left to right. Left-to-right calculation should be emphasized in this lesson.

Ask students working individually or in pairs to take out their money pouches. Have students place $234 on their desks with hundreds on the left and ones on the right. Below the $234 have students place $124.

2 hundreds	3 tens	4 ones
1 hundred	2 tens	4 ones

"When we add two numbers we combine them; that is, we count how many there are altogether."

First exercise: Ask students to add $234 and $124 by putting together the $100 bills, then the $10 bills, and then the $1 bills.

3 hundreds	5 tens	8 ones

"With our money we have added $234 and $124. By counting the bills we can find the sum."

"How many $100 bills are there?" 3 *"How much money is that?"* $300

"How many $10 bills are there?" 5 *"How much money is that?"* $50

"How much money have we counted so far?" $350

"How many $1 bills are there?" 8 *"How much money is that?"* $8

"How much money is there in all?" $358

"Now separate the money again into $234 and $124. This time we will count the bills without moving them together."

"Altogether, how many $100 bills do you see?" 3

"How many $10 bills do you see?" 5

"How many $1 bills do you see?" 8

"How much money do you see in all?" $358

"Now close your eyes and try to see the money on your desk using your imagination. You should see $234 spread out on your desk and $124 spread out below that."

"With your eyes shut, think about the $100 bills."

"How many are there?" 2 and 1, which is 3

"How much money is that?" $300

"Remember $300."

"Now think about the $10 bills. How many are there?" 3 and 2, which is 5

"How much money is that?" $50

"We put $300 and $50 together and remember $350."

"Now think about the $1 bills. How many are there?" 4 and 4, which is 8

"So how much money is there altogether?" $358

"Open your eyes. Could you imagine the money?"

Second exercise: Have students clear their desks.

"Let's do this again by adding $356 and $212. Place $356 on your desk and place $212 below it. This time we will not move the bills together; we will just count them."

Have students count 100's, 10's, and 1's. Then have them repeat the process with their eyes closed.

Third exercise: Repeat the activity one more time adding $350 and $125.

Activity 11 **Addition with Exchange**

Review

daily almanac activities

mental math

- How many days are in a common year? In a leap year?
- Count leap years from '00 through '96.
- Nickels: Count up and down between 5¢ and one dollar.
- Dimes: Count up and down between 10¢ and two dollars.
- Quarters: Count up and down between 25¢ and two dollars.
- Twenties: Count up and down between $20 and $100.
- Imagine placing $124 on your desk. Imagine placing $250 below that. Mentally count the bills. Altogether, how much money is there?   *$374*

Materials Needed

- Play money for $1, $10, and $100 bills

Activity

Students will combine amounts of money to illustrate addition. Today's activity requires students to exchange bills (regroup) when the number of bills in a denomination is ten or more.

First exercise: Ask students to take out their money pouches. Have students place $235 and $356 on their desks.

"To physically add $235 and $356, we move the bills together to make one amount of money."

"Put the $100 bills together. Put the $10 bills together. Put the $1 bills together."

5	8	11

"How many $100 bills are there?"   *5*   *"What is the value?"*   *$500*

"How many $10 bills are there?"   *8*   *"What is the value?"*   *$80*

"How many $1 bills are there?"   *11*   *"What is the value?"*   *$11*

"How much money is there in all?"   *$591*

"It looks like 'five hundred eighty-eleven' dollars."

"How can we make it look like $591?"   We exchange ten $1 bills for one $10 bill.   *"Exchange with the 'bank.' Your money pouch is the bank. Put the $10*

bill from the bank with the other $10 bills. Now there are nine $10 bills and there is one $1 bill."

5	9	1

Second exercise: Ask students to clear their desks to start a new exercise. *"We will add two more amounts of money. This time add $163 and $360. Place $163 on your desk and below that place $360. Then move them together to add."*

4	12	3

"How much money is this?" (From left to right the mental calculation goes, "Four hundred ... five hundred ... five hundred twenty-three.") *"To show the sum with bills, we need to exchange ten $10 bills for one $100 bill. Exchange with the bank and place the $100 bill with the other hundreds."*

5	2	3

Third exercise: Have students clear their desks. *"Let's add again. This time we will exchange twice. Add $375 and $268. Move the bills together."*

5	13	13

"How much money is this?" (From left to right the mental calculation goes, "Five hundred ... six hundred ... six hundred thirty ... six hundred forty ... three.") *"To show the sum with bills, we need to exchange twice. We exchange ten $10 bills for one $100 bill, and we exchange ten $1 bills for one $10 bill. Exchange with the bank and place the bills in the proper piles. Now how much money do you see?"* *$643*

6	4	3

Fourth exercise: Have the students try adding $375 and $486 without guidance. *$861*

Activity 12   # Mental Addition with Exchange

Review

daily almanac activities

mental math

- Count up and down by 2's between 2 and 32.

- At what temperatures does water freeze and boil on the Fahrenheit and Celsius scales?

- Nickels: Count up and down by 5's between 5 and 100.

- Dimes: Count by 10's from 25 to 95 (25, 35, 45, …).

- Quarters: How much money is 2, 3, 5, 6, and 7 quarters?

- Imagine placing $312 on your desk. Imagine placing $525 below that. Mentally count the bills. Altogether, how much money is there?   *$837*

Materials Needed

- Play money for $1, $10, and $100 bills

Activity

While reviewing addition with exchange taught in Activity 11, students will practice mental addition with exchange (regrouping).

First exercise: Ask students to take out their money pouches. Have students use their money to add $380 and $275, but wait to exchange. When the bills are moved together, there are:

5 hundreds	15 tens	5 ones

Select students to methodically describe the exchange process and to predict how many of each type of bill there will be after the exchange takes place. Gain a class consensus and then have the students perform the exchange.

6 hundreds	5 tens	5 ones

Second exercise: Next, have the students add $375 and $275. Again have students wait to exchange. After moving the bills together, there should be:

5 hundreds   14 tens   10 ones

Select students to describe the exchange that will take place and to predict how many of each type of bill there will be after the exchange. When agreement is reached, have the students perform the exchange.

6 hundreds   5 tens   no ones

Third exercise: Ask students to perform the next addition using their imaginations.

"Imagine placing $360 on your desk."

"Imagine placing $385 below that. Mentally count the bills."

"How many hundreds are there?" *6*

"How many tens are there?" *14*

"How many ones are there?" *5*

"Which bills need to be exchanged?" *Exchange 10 tens for 1 hundred.*

"Then how many hundreds, tens, and ones will there be?" *There will be 7 hundreds, 4 tens, and 5 ones.*

"How much is that?" *$745*

Fourth exercise: Ask students to perform one more addition using their imaginations. Write $456 and $275 on the board. Students may want to view the numbers as they mentally calculate. Ask the students to imagine using their money to add $456 and $275. Mentally count the bills.

"How many hundreds are there?" *6*

"How many tens are there?" *12*

"If 10 tens are exchanged, how many hundreds and tens will there be?" *There will be 7 hundreds and 2 tens.*

"How many ones are there?" *11*

"If 10 ones are exchanged, how many tens and ones will there be?" *There will be 3 tens and 1 one.*

"Altogether, how much money is there?" *$731*

Activity 13   **Using Money to Subtract**

Review

daily almanac activities

mental math

- Count by 7's and by 12's to 84.

- Which months have exactly 30 days?

- Nickels: How much money is 3, 5, 7, and 10 nickels?

- Dimes: Count by 10's from 5 to 95 (5, 15, 25, …).

- Quarters: How much money is 3, 4, 6, 8, and 9 quarters?

- Imagine using your money to add $275 and $250. Mentally count the bills. Exchange if necessary. Altogether, how much money is there? *$525*

Materials Needed

- Play money for $1, $10, and $100 bills

Activity

Students will use money to illustrate subtraction without exchange. Students should gain a kinesthetic sense of moving quantities together with addition and moving quantities apart with subtraction. Again, emphasize working left to right.

First exercise: Ask students to put $475 on their desks.

> *"Today we will use money to subtract. We are starting with $475. We are going to subtract $123 from $475. Pull $123 from the $475 that is on your desk. Move the $123 so that it is below the remaining bills."*

3 hundreds   5 tens   2 ones   remain

1 hundred   2 tens   3 ones   subtracted

> *"Count the remaining bills. How much of the $475 is left?"*   *$352*

"We now have two amounts of money on the desk: $123 and $352. How can we get back to $475?"   We get back to $475 by adding $123 and $352.

"Move $123 and $352 together so that we have $475 again."

Second exercise: *"This time subtract $260 from $475. Pull $260 from $475 and move the $260 below the remaining bills."*

<table>
<tr><td>2 hundreds</td><td>1 ten</td><td>5 ones</td><td>remain</td></tr>
</table>

<table>
<tr><td>2 hundreds</td><td>6 tens</td><td></td><td>subtracted</td></tr>
</table>

"Count the bills that remain. How much money is left when $260 is subtracted from $475?"   *$215*

"If we add $260 and $215, what will be the sum?"   *$475*

"Move $260 and $215 together so that we have $475 again."

Third exercise: *"This time we will imagine the subtraction before we move any money."*

"Imagine subtracting $155 from $475. Think about how many bills will be left. Does anybody want to predict how much of the $475 remains after $155 is pulled away?"   *$320*

"Test your prediction by subtracting $155 from $475 and counting the bills that remain."

<table>
<tr><td>3 hundreds</td><td>2 tens</td><td>remain</td></tr>
</table>

<table>
<tr><td>1 hundred</td><td>5 tens</td><td>5 ones</td><td>subtracted</td></tr>
</table>

"When $155 is subtracted from $475, how much money remains?"   *$320*

"If we add $155 and $320, what is the sum?"   *$475*

This activity may be continued as time allows.

Activity 14   **Counting Coins**

Review

daily almanac activities

mental math

- Count up and down by 2's between 2 and 32.

- Count up by dimes from 25¢ to $1.25.

- Count up by quarters from 25¢ to $3.00.

- At what temperatures does water freeze and boil on the Fahrenheit and Celsius scales?

- How many days are in a common year? In a leap year?

- Count leap years from '00 through '96.

- Imagine using your money to add $360 and $275. Mentally count the bills and exchange, if necessary. Altogether, how much money is this?   *$635*

- Imagine using money to subtract $124 from $275. How much money is left?   *$151*

problem solving

- What is the date two weeks after September 3?   *September 17*

- What month is half a year after May?   *November*

- What month is half a year before May?   *November*

Materials Needed for Activity A

- A copy of "Counting Coins" (Master 6) for each student or each small group of students, or one overhead transparency of Master 6

Materials Needed for Activity B

- One small paper cup containing various coins for each group of students (Number the cups to distinguish them.)

Activity

In these activities students will practice counting coins. Emphasize beginning the count with the largest denominations and ending with the smallest denominations. Students may begin counting coin by coin. Soon some may begin counting groups of coins. Encourage explanations of successful strategies.

Activity A uses an activity sheet (Master 6) to provide practice counting coins. Activity B requires coins and a coin cup to be provided by the teacher for each group of students. Feel free to choose either or both activities. Students may want to work ahead on Activity A. If you prefer that the class work together and discuss one exercise at a time, have students turn the activity sheet upside down and fold up one third of the page at a time, or simply project each exercise using an overhead transparency.

Activity A: Have students work through each of the three exercises. It may be helpful for students to draw a line through coins they have counted. Examples of counts across the bottom of Exercise 1 include:

25¢, 50¢, 60¢, 70¢, 80¢, 85¢, 86¢, 87¢, 88¢, 89¢   or

50¢, 80¢, 85¢, 89¢

Activity B: Arrange students in small groups. Provide a small, numbered paper cup with various coins for each group. Have each group record the number of the cup and the counted value of the coins in that cup. Rotate the cups through the groups until all groups have counted the coins in all the cups. One person in each group may count the coins in a cup while others watch or assist. When a group gets a new cup, they select a new counter. Encourage counting larger coins first. Also, encourage physically moving and grouping the coins as each count proceeds.

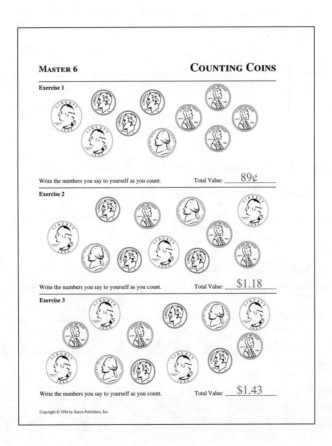

Activity 15   **Sums of a Dollar**

Review

daily almanac activities

mental math

- Count by 7's and by 12's to 84.

- Which months have 31 days?

- How much money is 3 quarters, 1 dime, 2 nickels, and 1 penny?

- Imagine adding $375 and $175. What is the sum?   *$550*

- Imagine using your money to subtract $125 from $275. How much money is left?   *$150*

problem solving

- Ryan turned ten years old in May. In what month will Ryan be ten and a half years old?   *November* (Counting strategy: Count six months from May.)

Materials Needed

- Ten pennies and ten dimes (or dime substitutes) for each student or pair of students

Activity

The purpose of this activity is to demonstrate a method to mentally calculate sums of one dollar. When purchases are made with whole dollars that require change to be returned, this method can be used to calculate how much change should be returned.

Ask students to place ten dimes and ten pennies on their desks.

"How much money is ten dimes and ten pennies?"   *$1.10*

"What are two ways we can make one dollar with these coins?"   *We can make $1.00 with 10 dimes or with 9 dimes and 10 pennies.*

"First we will practice making a dollar with just dimes. Move one dime to the center of your desk. How many more dimes do you need to move to make a dollar?"   *9 dimes*

"Show one dime plus nine dimes on your desk."

Write "1 dime + 9 dimes" on the board. Then repeat the question starting with 2, 3, 4, and 5 dimes, writing each pair on the board.

1 dime	2 dimes	3 dimes	4 dimes	5 dimes
+ 9 dimes	+ 8 dimes	+ 7 dimes	+ 6 dimes	+ 5 dimes
10 dimes	10 dimes	10 dimes	10 dimes	10 dimes

"Now we will practice making a dollar with dimes and pennies. We will use ten pennies. How many dimes will we need?"   *9 dimes*

"Move one dime and one penny to the center of your desk. How many dimes and how many pennies do you need to move to make a dollar?"   *8 dimes and 9 pennies*

"Altogether, how many dimes and how many pennies are there?"   *Nine dimes plus ten pennies equals one dollar.*

Write the following on the board:

$$
\begin{array}{rl}
1\ \text{dime} \quad 1\ \text{penny} & \$0.11 \\
+\ 8\ \text{dimes} \quad 9\ \text{pennies} & +\ \$0.89 \\
\hline
9\ \text{dimes}\ 10\ \text{pennies} & \$1.00 \\
\end{array}
$$

"This time, move three dimes and six pennies to the center of your desk. How much money is this?"   *$0.36*

"How many dimes and pennies do we need to move to make a dollar?"   *6 dimes and 4 pennies*

"How much money is six dimes and four pennies?"   *$0.64*

"Altogether, how many dimes and pennies are there?"   *Nine dimes plus ten pennies equals one dollar.*

Write the following on the board:

$$
\begin{array}{rl}
3\ \text{dimes} \quad 6\ \text{pennies} & \$0.36 \\
+\ 6\ \text{dimes} \quad 4\ \text{pennies} & +\ \$0.64 \\
\hline
9\ \text{dimes}\ 10\ \text{pennies} & \$1.00 \\
\end{array}
$$

"Now move 47 cents to the center of your desk. How many dimes and pennies did you use?"   *4 dimes and 7 pennies*

"How many more dimes and pennies do you need to move to make a dollar?"   *5 dimes and 3 pennies*

"How much money is five dimes and three pennies?"   *$0.53*

"Altogether, how many dimes and pennies are there?"   *Nine dimes plus ten pennies equals one dollar.*

Write the following on the board:

$$
\begin{array}{rl}
4\ \text{dimes} \quad 7\ \text{pennies} & \$0.47 \\
+\ 5\ \text{dimes} \quad 3\ \text{pennies} & +\ \$0.53 \\
\hline
9\ \text{dimes}\ 10\ \text{pennies} & \$1.00 \\
\end{array}
$$

"Try some problems mentally. Remember, a dollar equals nine dimes plus ten pennies."

Dan has 27¢. How much more money does Dan need to have a dollar?   *73¢*

The pencil cost 38¢. Jan paid for it with a dollar bill. How much money should she get back?   *62¢*

Activity 16   # Subtraction with Exchange

Review

daily almanac activities

mental math

- Count by 7's and by 12's to 84.

- Count leap years from '00 through '96.

- At what temperatures on the Fahrenheit and Celsius scales does water freeze and boil?

- Imagine using money to subtract $240 from $476. How much money is left?   *$236*

- How much money is 2 quarters, 3 dimes, 3 nickels, and 2 pennies?   *97¢*

- Simon paid a dollar for an apple that cost 35¢. How much money should Simon get back?   *65¢*

- How many quarters equal one dollar? Two dollars? Three dollars?

problem solving

- Natalie turned eleven years old in August. In what month will she be eleven and a half years old?   *February* (Counting strategy: Count six months from August.)

Materials Needed

- Play money for $1, $10, and $100 bills

Activity

Today's activity, "Subtraction with Exchange," requires children to exchange bills before completing the subtraction.

First exercise: *"We will be using money to subtract again. Today we will need to exchange bills before we subtract. Put six $10 bills on your desk. How much money is this?"*   *$60*

"From $60 we will subtract $36. That means we need to pull three tens and six ones from the $60 on the desk. Since there are no ones on the desk, how can we complete this subtraction?"

We exchange one ten from $60 for ten ones. After the exchange, we have five tens and ten ones, which is still $60.

"Now we can pull three tens and six ones from the desk. How much money is left?"   *$24*

Second exercise: Ask students to put $82 on their desks. *"We are going to subtract $65 from $82. That means we need to pull six tens and five ones from $82. We can take six tens, but how can we take five ones?"*

> *We can exchange one ten from $82 for ten ones. Now we have seven tens and twelve ones. Seven tens and twelve ones is still $82.*

"Now we can subtract $65 from $82."

"How much money is left?"   *$17*

Third exercise: Ask students to put $324 on their desks. *"We are going to subtract $163. Do we have enough bills to subtract?"*

> *No, we do not have enough $10 bills.*

"This time we need to exchange a $100 bill for $10 bills. What do we do?"

> *We exchange a $100 bill from $324 for ten $10 bills. After the exchange, we have two hundreds, twelve tens, and four ones, which is $324.*

"Now subtract $163. How much money is left?"   *$161*

Activity 17   **Selecting Coins for Change**

Review

daily almanac activities

mental math

- Count by 7's from 7 through 84.

- How many weeks and days are there from the 3rd to the 25th?   *3 weeks, 1 day*

- Imagine adding $365 and $366. What is the sum?   *$731*

- Imagine subtracting $56 from $80. How much money is left?   *$24*

problem solving: (Search for easiest approach.)

- Five quarters, five dimes, and five nickels all together equal how many quarters? (How many quarters equal five dimes? Five nickels?)

Materials Needed

Each pair or group of students needs:

- Several "price tags" (e.g., 62¢, 70¢, $0.39, $0.53)

- Play money $1 bills

- Coin cup containing three quarters, three dimes, three nickels, and five pennies

Activity

*Students will practice mentally calculating change for a dollar. Then students will count back coins, beginning with the largest denomination of coin possible. (Note: This method differs from the method of counting **from** the price **toward** the amount tendered, which begins counting with the lowest denomination coins.)*

Arrange students in pairs or small groups of three or four. Have one student in each group play the role of sales clerk while the others play the role of customers. One customer selects a price tag and presents that price tag and a $1 bill to the clerk. Together, they agree on the amount of change the customer should get back. Then the clerk counts change back to the customer, beginning with the largest denomination coin. The customer then assumes the role of sales clerk, returning the coins to the coin cup while another customer selects a purchase. Allow sufficient time for all children to play both roles.

Example: The customer selects a price tag of 63¢ and presents the tag and a dollar bill to the sales clerk. After mental calculation, both agree that 37¢ change is due the customer. The sales clerk selects coins totaling 37¢ by first taking a quarter for 25¢, then a dime making 35¢, and then two pennies for a total of 37¢.

Activity 18   **Subtraction with Two Exchanges**

Review

daily almanac activities

mental math

- Count by quarters to $3.00.
- Imagine adding $225 and $375. What is the sum?   *$600*
- Imagine subtracting $120 from $300. How much money is left?   *$180*

problem solving: (Look beyond typical borders.)

- July and August are consecutive months (two months "in a row") that have 31 days. Name two other consecutive months that have 31 days.   *December and January*

Materials Needed

- Play money for $1, $10, and $100 bills

Activity

Today's activity extends subtraction with exchange to include two exchanges. Allow students to experiment with the order of exchanges.

First exercise (one exchange): Ask students to place $306 on their desk and to subtract $134 from that.

> ***"What denomination of bills do we need to be able to subtract?"***   *tens*

> ***"How will we get the tens?"***   *Exchange one hundred for ten tens.*

> ***"Pull $134 from $306. How much money is left?"***   *$172*

Second exercise (two exchanges): Ask students to place $642 on their desks.

> ***"We are going to subtract $358 from $642. What denomination of bills do we need to be able to subtract?"***   *More tens and more ones are needed.*

> ***"How will we get more tens and more ones?"***   *Exchange one hundred for ten tens and one ten for ten ones.*

> ***"Exchange bills. Who exchanged for ones first? Who exchanged for tens first? How many of each denomination do you have?"***   *There will be five hundreds, thirteen tens, and twelve ones, which is still equal to $642.*

> ***"Pull $358 from $642. How much money is left?"***   *$284*

Third exercise: Ask students to place $503 on their desks and to subtract $136. For this exercise, students will need to exchange for tens before exchanging for ones. Monitor the students' activities.   *$367*

Activity 19   **Writing Checks**

Review

daily almanac activities

mental math

- Count by 7's and by 12's to 84.

- How much money is 5 quarters, 4 dimes, 3 nickels, and 2 pennies? *$1.82*

- If you pay a dollar for an item that costs 39¢, how much money should you get back? What coins should you get back? *61¢; 2 quarters, 1 dime, 1 penny*

- What temperature on the Fahrenheit scale is the same temperature as 0° on the Celsius scale? *32°F*

- How many weeks and days are there from the 3rd to the 21st? *2 weeks, 4 days*

- Imagine adding $290 and $210. What is the sum? *$500*

- Imagine subtracting $124 from $360. How much is left? *$236*

problem solving: (Make a list.)

- What month is halfway between June and February? *October*

Materials Needed

- A copy of "Writing Checks" (Master 7) for each student
(Additional copies of the master may be copied and available for subsequent review.)

Activity

Writing checks provides students with a "grown-up" activity that relates decimal and fraction notation. This relationship should be emphasized during the activity.

First exercise: Distribute Master 7, "Writing Checks," to each student. Point out the five required and one optional sections of a check to be completed.

> Required: full date (effective date of check)
> name of payee
> dollar amount as a numeral, cents as a decimal
> dollar amount in words, cents as a fraction
> signature of payer

> Optional: memo

Have students write a check to *Bargain Toys* for $44.36, using today's date. Illustrate the proper spelling, including hyphenation and the fraction form for cents.

Forty-four and 36/100 dollars

Have students sign their names.

Second exercise: Ask students to write a check to *Growell Grocers* for $115.00. You may select a month for the check that you would like students to practice spelling. Monitor student efforts.

<u>*One hundred fifteen and no/100*</u> dollars

Third exercise: Have students write a check to *Home Mortgage* for $829.07.

<u>*Eight hundred twenty-nine and 07/100*</u> dollars

UNIT 3   FROM HERE TO THERE

"From Here to There" is an integrated unit that incorporates writing and concepts from geography with a variety of mathematical concepts to involve students in orienting themselves to the world around them. Students are asked to read and create maps, to use compass directions when interpreting or drawing a map, to follow and formulate oral and written directions, to employ tools and estimation when measuring distances, to work with scale when finding distances between cities on a United States map (Master 8), and to sketch maps as a problem-solving strategy.

Looking ahead, preparation for some activities may be necessary. Materials needed in this unit include magnetic compasses (Activity 21) and butcher paper and markers for making wall maps (Activities 23 and 26). Activity 26 encourages a walking activity. Permission may need to be secured if an off-campus walk is planned. The sketch and written directions for Activity 20 and Activity 29 may provide samples for inclusion in a student portfolio.

Activity 20   Sketching a Map

Review

daily almanac activities

mental math

- Count up and down by 5's between 5 and 100.

- Count by quarters to $3.00.

- How much money is 4 quarters, 4 dimes, and 4 nickels?   *$1.60*

- How many weeks and days are there from the 5th to the 22nd? How many days is that? *2 weeks, 3 days; 17 days*

- If you pay a dollar for an item that costs 43¢, how much money should you get back? What coins should you get back?   *57¢; 2 quarters, 1 nickel, 2 pennies*

- Imagine adding $350 and $350. What is the sum?   *$700*

- Imagine subtracting $160 from $300. How much is left?   *$140*

problem solving: (Look for a pattern.)

• Post this partial list of the multiples of 9 on the board:

9

18

27

36

Counting by 9's, the first four numbers are 9, 18, 27, and 36. Look for a pattern in these numbers. Then continue the list to 90.

Activity

As the initial activity in this unit, students will sketch a map showing the location of school and their home. Students will also provide written directions describing to a friend how to get to their home from school. This initial effort should be completed without assistance and should be collected to provide a basis for assessing student learning during this unit.

"Imagine that you want to invite a friend from school to come to your home. Your friend does not know where you live, so you need to provide directions that your friend can follow."

"Sketch a map showing the route you travel on your way home from school. Use line segments to show streets. Write the names of the streets you remember. Draw a rectangle on the map to show the location of the school and another rectangle to show where you live."

"After drawing the map, provide written directions that describe how to get to your home from school."

Activity 21   **Compass Directions**

Review

daily almanac activities

mental math

- Count by 9's from 9 to 90.

- Count by 10's from 1 to 101.   *1, 11, 21, 31, ...*

- One dollar is equal to how many quarters? How many dimes? How many nickels? *4 quarters; 10 dimes; 20 nickels*

- Count by half dollars from half a dollar to five dollars.   *Half a dollar, one dollar, one and one half dollars, two dollars, ...*

- If you pay $1.00 for an item that costs 64¢, how much money should you get back? What coins should you get back?   *36¢; 1 quarter, 1 dime, 1 penny*

- Imagine adding $256 and $135. What is the sum?   *$391*

- Imagine subtracting $54 from $92. How much is left?   *$38*

problem solving

- What month is halfway between May and March?   *October*

Materials Needed

- A copy of the United States map (Master 8) for each student (This map will be needed throughout the unit.)

- A wall map of the United States would be helpful.

- A magnetic compass for each student or each pair or small group of students

- Plastic sleeves for storing the maps are recommended.

Activity

Distribute magnetic compasses. Students should hold the compass level so that the needle is free to move. Have students identify the magnetized end of the needle. Away from a local magnetic field, the needle of a compass points north. Have students gradually turn the compass so that north (N) on the face of the compass is in alignment with the north-pointing needle. Ask students what S, W, and E abbreviate.

The "you are here" location when reading a compass is the center of the compass. Ask students to imagine that they are at the center of the compass. Have them point to the north, to the south, to the east, and to the west.

Have students identify the direction from which the sun rises and the direction in which it sets.

Ask students to name landmarks that lie to the north, south, east, and west.

The direction between north and east is northeast (NE). Have students point to the northeast, to the northwest, to the southeast, and to the southwest.

Ask students to think about where their homes are. Ask them to point toward their homes. Ask volunteers to name the direction to their home from school.

Distribute a "United States Map" (Master 8) to each student. Point out that maps are usually drawn so that the top of the map is north. The compass graphic on the map confirms that this map is drawn in the usual orientation.

Have students find their present location on the map. Ask students to name cities, states, countries, or bodies of water on the map that are north, east, south, and west of their current location.

Have students stand and face north, holding the map so that the compass graphic on the map actually points north. Then have students point in the direction of the Atlantic Ocean, the Pacific Ocean, the Gulf of Mexico, and various states, cities, countries, or features of the teacher's choosing.

Activity 22 **Giving Directions**

Review

daily almanac activities

mental math

- Count by 9's from 9 to 99.

- Count by 10's from 2 to 102.   *2, 12, 22, ...*

- Count by quarters from 25¢ to $3.00.

- Two dollars is equal to how many quarters? How many dimes? How many nickels? *8 quarters; 20 dimes; 40 nickels*

- Point to the north, to the south, to the east, and to the west.

- Which direction is opposite to north? Opposite to west? Opposite to northeast? Opposite to southeast?

- Imagine adding $236 and $246. What is the sum?   *$482*

- Imagine subtracting $140 from $200. How much is left?   *$60*

problem solving

- Ask the students to draw a sketch as the problem is read:

  Trihn started on a walk. She walked two blocks north, then four blocks east, then three blocks south, and then one block west. Then Trihn decided to return to where she started her walk. Write directions for Trihn to follow to return to where she started.

- Ask volunteers to provide alternate solutions.

Materials Needed

- A copy of "Neighborhood Map" (Master 9) or similar map appropriate for the activity for each student

Activity

Arranged in pairs or small groups, students will take turns giving oral directions from one site on the map to another. After oral practice, students will write directions from one site to another.

Arrange students in groups of two, three, or four. Distribute neighborhood maps to each student. Demonstrate the activity for students by selecting a site on the map and orally giving directions to another site on the map while students mentally trace the described route.

Example: *"Starting from school, travel north on Knox two blocks to Monroe. Turn east on Monroe to Hamilton and north on Hamilton to Quincy. Whose house is on the southeast corner?"*

Have each student select a starting site and describe a route to another site as the other members of the group follow the description. As the activity proceeds, some students may devise circuitous routes to sites which could be reached following a simpler route. Perceiving alternate routes is a mathematical ability worth developing. Following involved directions can be an amusing way for the other members of the group to practice directional skills.

After students have practiced giving directions orally, have each student give written directions from one site to another. Either prescribe the starting and ending sites, or have students select their own.

Activity 23   # Local Map

Review

daily almanac activities

mental math

- Count by 9's from 9 to 99.

- Count by 7's and by 12's to 84.

- How many quarters is half a dollar? One and one half dollars?   *2 quarters; 6 quarters*

- Point west, south, north, and east.

- Which direction is opposite to west? To southwest?

- Imagine adding $65 and $56. What is the sum?   *$121*

- Imagine subtracting $36 from $100. How much is left?   *$64*

problem solving

- Draw a sketch of this story:

  > Pedro started his walk. He walked one block north, then four blocks east, and then three blocks south.

  Write two sets of directions that Pedro could follow to return to where he started.

Materials Needed

- A sheet of butcher paper or other large paper for drawing a map large enough for the class to see (1 sheet per group)

- Markers for drawing and labeling the maps

- Rulers or metersticks for drawing line segments

- Masking tape for posting the maps

Activity

Review which direction from school is north. Arrange students in small groups and provide each group with a large sheet of paper for drawing a local map. Suggest that they orient themselves so that they are facing north with the paper in front of them.

Have students use pencils to lightly sketch the street arrangement in the immediate neighborhood of the school. Monitor and assist group efforts. When a pencil sketch is satisfactory, provide markers for the group to darken and label the map for posting. Besides drawing and naming streets, students may identify the location of the school, nearby homes, and parks, theaters, or other prominent sites in the immediate area. Ask students to draw a compass graphic on the map before posting.

Post the maps around the room and discuss with the class similarities and differences between the maps. Are all the maps oriented with north to the top? Begin identifying differences in scale. Which map is drawn with the largest/smallest scale? Which map seems to be drawn closest to a consistent scale? Which features on other maps seem to have a distorted scale? What makes a map a useful map?

Activity 24   **Inch Scale**

Review

daily almanac activities

mental math

- Count by 12's from 12 to 96.

- There are 12 inches in one foot. How many inches are in two feet? Three feet? Four feet?

- Count by 9's from 9 to 99.

- Point to the northwest, northeast, southwest, and southeast.

- From the 4th to the 27th is how many weeks and days? How many days is that?   *3 weeks, 2 days; 23 days*

problem solving

- What month is halfway between July and March?   *November*

Materials Needed

- A one-foot ruler for each student

- A one-inch by twelve-inch strip of card stock or unlined tagboard for each student (with extras available)

- A copy of "United States Map" (Master 8) for each student, distributed in Activity 21

Activity

In this activity students will work individually to make their own twelve-inch rulers for use during the balance of the unit. These student-made rulers will be marked to show halves and quarters. Demonstrating this activity with a transparency on an overhead or with an overscale display on the chalkboard is helpful. Students will use their rulers to measure the distances between cities on their U.S. maps.

Distribute the strips of card stock and rulers to students. If students are using dual-scale rulers, emphasize that this activity uses the inch scale.

Have students lay the inch-scale ruler on top of the strip of paper, matching the left ends of each. They should slide the ruler toward them a little so that they can mark the strip of paper.

At each long inch mark on the ruler, have students make a mark on the strip of paper. When they have made a mark for each inch, they should remove the ruler and number the inch marks.

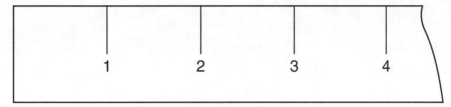

Strip of paper with inches marked

Then have the students set the ruler aside and use just a pencil and the strip of paper. Ask students to judge the halfway point between the inch marks and to make a mark at each halfway point. The marks should be a little shorter than the inch marks. These are the half-inch marks.

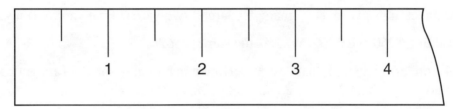

Strip of paper with half-inches marked

Have students point to each mark, starting from the left, and count in unison, "One half, one, one and one half, two, …."

Ask students to make one more set of marks on the strip of paper. Have students judge the halfway point between each pair of marks and make marks not quite as long as the half-inch marks. The new marks are quarter-inch marks.

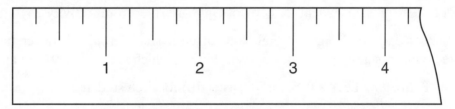

Strip of paper with quarter-inches marked

Have students point to each mark, starting from the left, and count, "One quarter, one half, three quarters, one, one and one quarter, one and one half, one and three quarters, two, …."

Ask students to place their United States maps on their desks so that they can measure the distances between cities. Using their paper-strip rulers, students should hold the upper left corner of the ruler on the dot for one city and rotate the ruler so that the scale touches the dot for the second city. After final adjustments, students should read the distance in inches between the cities to the nearest mark on their rulers (to the nearest quarter inch).

Have students measure the distance in inches between:

- Los Angeles and Denver   *2 in.*
- Dallas and Chicago   *2 in.*
- Indianapolis and New York City   *$1\frac{3}{4}$ in.*

Activity 25   **Feet and Yards**

Review

daily almanac activities

mental math

- Count by 12's from 12 to 96.

- How many inches are in two feet? Three feet? Five feet?

- Count by 3's from 3 to 36.

- There are 3 feet in one yard. How many feet are in two yards? Five yards? Ten yards?

- Imagine adding $260 and $360. What is the sum?   *$620*

- Tara paid a dollar for an item that cost 38¢. How much money should Tara get back? What coins should she get back?   *62¢; 2 quarters, 1 dime, 2 pennies*

- On your United States map, how far in inches is it from Seattle to San Francisco?   *$1\frac{3}{4}$ in.*

problem solving

- Shannon ran 4 blocks west, 3 blocks south, 5 blocks east, and 6 blocks north. Write directions for Shannon to follow to return to her starting point.

Materials Needed

- A one-foot ruler for each student (or copy of tagboard ruler from Activity 24)

- A yardstick or one-yard length of tagboard for each small group (A meterstick may be substituted with masking tape at the one-yard length, which is between 91 cm and 92 cm.)

- A copy of "Estimating Feet and Yards" (Master 10) for each student

Activity

Arrange students in groups of three or four for this activity. Have students lay three one-foot rulers end to end so that they extend one yard. Each student should practice taking a big step that is one yard long. The step should be measured from heel to heel or from toe to toe, but not from toe to heel.

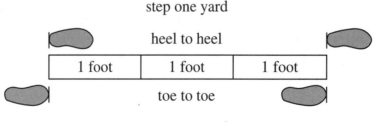

step one yard

heel to heel

| 1 foot | 1 foot | 1 foot |

toe to toe

step one yard

When students have practiced taking a one-yard step and have a "feel" for it, distribute the activity sheet "Estimating Feet and Yards" (Master 10) to each student. The children will hone their skill of estimating distances in feet and yards by "stepping off" the length and width of the classroom.

Distinguish length, the longer dimension, from width, the shorter dimension. After each estimate, students should use their rulers and yardsticks to measure the distance to the nearest foot. The "stepping off" estimates should be performed by each student. The ruler measurements may be a group effort as they "leap-frog" their rulers or slide the yardstick across the room.

Have students complete the activity sheet at home by selecting a room at home to measure.

Activity 26   **Miles**

Review

daily almanac activities

mental math

- Count by 7's to 84.

- Count by 9's to 99.

- Count by 10's from 3 to 103.

- Point to the southeast, northeast, southwest, and northwest.

- How many inches is one foot? Two feet? Three feet?

- Which months have exactly 30 days?

- Which direction would you need to travel going from Kansas to South Dakota?

- On your United States map, how many inches is it from Pittsburgh to Omaha?   *2 in.*

- Count by fourths on the inch ruler from $\frac{1}{4}$ to 3.   *$\frac{1}{4}$, $\frac{1}{2}$, $\frac{3}{4}$, 1, 1$\frac{1}{4}$, 1$\frac{1}{2}$, 1$\frac{3}{4}$, 2, 2$\frac{1}{4}$, 2$\frac{1}{2}$, 2$\frac{3}{4}$, 3*

problem solving

- Neil drove six blocks east, then seven blocks south, then two blocks west, and then one block north. Write two different sets of directions Neil could follow to return to where he started.

Materials Needed

- Butcher paper or other large paper for drawing a map large enough for the class to see (The chalkboard or an overhead transparency may be substituted, if necessary.)

Activity

As the United States gradually moves toward the metric system, evidence of the U.S. Customary System–formerly the English System–remains carved into our landscape. Throughout the west and midwest especially, land was sectioned for settlers in square mile parcels. Boundaries became roads, and in many cities, towns, and rural areas, main roads lie one mile apart. This activity will provide students with a physical sense of a one-mile distance as well as a review of the feet and yard equivalents for one mile.

"We have used inches, feet, and yards to measure distances. If we drive a long distance, what units do we use to measure how far we have traveled?"   *miles*

Making a Map

Post paper for sketching a map. Sketch the location of the school near the center of the paper.

"Can you think of any buildings, streets, or other landmarks that are about a mile from school? Does anyone live about a mile from school?"

As students offer suggestions, sketch a map that shows the location of sites about one mile from the school.

Taking a Walk

"If you walked a mile, how many steps do you think you would take?"

List student suggestions, and then write "1760 yards" on the chalkboard.

"A mile is 1760 yards. When we walk we usually take steps that are smaller than one yard. Does that help you guess how many steps you might take in a mile?"

Consider the following one-mile-walk options:

1. Plan a one-mile walk on campus during physical education. A one-mile walk takes about 20 minutes.

2. Plan a walking field trip to a destination such as a library, museum, monument, or produce store that is a half mile or farther away.

Students may want to time the one-mile walk. Some children may even want to count their steps.

Activity 27   **Scale on the United States Map**

Review

daily almanac activities

mental math

- Count by 3's from 3 to 30.

- How many feet are in one yard? Two yards? Three yards?   *3; 6; 9*

- How many inches are in two feet? Three feet? Four feet?

- How many days are in two weeks? Three weeks? Four weeks?

- Count by fourths from 2 inches to 4 inches.   *2, $2\frac{1}{4}$, $2\frac{1}{2}$, $2\frac{3}{4}$, 3, $3\frac{1}{4}$, $3\frac{1}{2}$, $3\frac{3}{4}$, 4*

- One mile is how many yards?   *1760 yards*

- How many inches is it from Miami to Indianapolis on your United States map?   *$2\frac{1}{2}$ in.*

problem solving

- There are 1760 yards in a mile. Figure out how many feet there are in a mile. (Since each yard is three feet, we may multiply 1760 by 3, or add 1760 + 1760 + 1760, to get 5280 feet.)

Materials Needed

- Each student needs his/her ruler and the United States map (Master 8) distributed in Activity 21.

Activity

Students will use their paper-strip rulers to measure the distances between cities. Then they will calculate the approximate number of miles between the cities using the map scale.

Students should have their United States map and their paper-strip rulers on their desks. Help students find the scale of the map. Ask students questions like the following:

"An inch on this map represents a distance of how far on the earth?"   *One inch represents 400 miles.*

"How many miles would be represented by two inches? Three inches?"   *800 miles; 1200 miles*

"How many miles would be represented by one quarter of an inch? By one half of an inch? By three quarters of an inch?"   *100 mi; 200 mi; 300 mi*

"How many inches on the map is it from Los Angeles to Denver?"   *2 in.*

"About how many miles is that?"   *800 mi*

"How did you figure out how many miles it was?"

"The drive from Los Angeles to Denver is close to 1000 miles. How can you explain the difference?"   On a map we can measure the straight-line distance between cities. However, the road between Los Angeles and Denver is not straight. The bends and turns in the road add many miles to the driving distance.

"How many inches on the map is it from Dallas to Chicago?"   2 in.

"About how many miles is that?"   800 mi

"How did you figure this out?"

"About how many miles is it from Atlanta to New York City?"   800 miles

Have pairs of students ask each other distances between cities on the map.

Activity 28   # Drawing Maps to Solve Problems

Review

daily almanac activities

mental math

- Count by 9's from 9 to 99.

- Count by 10's from 4 to 104.

- How many days is three weeks? Four weeks? Five weeks?

- How many inches is three feet? Four feet? Five feet?

- How many feet is two yards? Three yards? Ten yards?

- Point to the south, west, north, and east.

- Ismael paid a dollar for an item that cost 58¢. How much money should he get back? What coins should he receive in change?   *42¢; 1 quarter, 1 dime, 1 nickel, 2 pennies*

- A mile is 1760 yards. How many feet is a mile?   *5280 feet*

- Count by fourths from $1\frac{1}{4}$ to $3\frac{1}{2}$.

Materials Needed

- Pencil and paper are sufficient for students. If the teacher would like to present the stories visually as well as orally, the three stories may be written on the chalkboard or on an overhead transparency.

Problem-Solving Activity

Drawing diagrams or maps is a problem-solving strategy that students will practice in these three story problems.

First story: *"Listen to this story. See if you are able to draw a map from the information you hear."*

Pasadena is on the road between Glendale and Azusa. Glendale is five miles west of Pasadena, and Azusa is 13 miles east of Pasadena.

Discuss how to draw the map.

"Can you find how far it is from Glendale to Azusa?"   *18 mi*

Second story: *"Sometimes drawing a map or a sketch can help you solve a problem. This next story does not give compass directions, but we can still draw a sketch. The sketch might not look like what an actual map of the towns and road would look like, but the sketch can still help us answer questions about the story. Listen to the story and make a sketch of the information you hear."*

Dickens is on the road from Ralls to Guthrie. From Ralls to Guthrie is 64 miles. From Ralls to Dickens is 33 miles.

Observe the sketch drawing. Here is one sketch that fits the information. Other orientations are permissible as long as Dickens is the middle town.

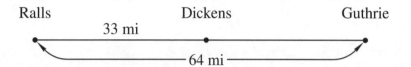

Ask volunteers whose sketches differ to draw their maps so that the class can see. Have the class determine if differing sketches have all the information.

"Some information is missing in this story. What question could we ask?"

"How many miles is it from Dickens to Guthrie?"   *31 mi*

"How did you find the answer?"

Third story: *"Here is one more problem. Draw a sketch that fits the information; then answer the question."*

From Yeso to Sumner is 22 miles. From Yeso through Sumner to Vaughn is 58 miles. How far is it from Sumner to Vaughn?

Here is one sketch that fits the information:

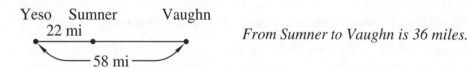

From Sumner to Vaughn is 36 miles.

Extension: Have students make a map and story problem for three make-believe towns. Have volunteers read their stories tomorrow.

Activity 29   **Maps and Written Directions**

Review

daily almanac activities

mental math

- A mile is how many yards? How many feet?

- At what temperatures does water freeze and boil on the Fahrenheit scale?

- Which months have exactly 30 days?

- Count by 7's to 84, and by 9's to 99.

- How many feet are in one yard? Two yards? Five yards?

- On your U.S. map, how many inches is it from Oklahoma City to Phoenix? About how many miles is that?   *$2\frac{1}{4}$ in.; 900 mi*

- Count by fourths from $2\frac{1}{2}$ to $4\frac{1}{2}$.

Materials Needed

- A copy of "Maps and Written Directions" (Master 11) for each student

Activity

In this activity students will practice making maps from written directions. They will also practice making written directions from maps.

"When people give you directions to their house, they may draw a map for you, or they may just use words to describe the route to take. We are going to practice drawing a map from written directions. We will also practice writing directions from a map."

Distribute the activity sheet "Maps and Written Directions" (Master 11) to each student. Read the directions in the first exercise, and then monitor students' work. Allow students to check one another's sketches. For the second exercise, ask volunteers to read the directions they have composed as the class evaluates the directions.

When the activity is completed, ask students to repeat the first activity of the unit (Activity 20).

"Sketch a map showing the route you travel on your way home from school. Use line segments to show streets. Write the names of the streets you remember. Draw a rectangle on the map to show the location of the school and another rectangle to show where you live."

"After drawing the map, make written directions that describe how to get to your home from school."

Unit 4   Estimation Investigation

Most of the activities in this unit revolve around a contest to guess the number of pennies in a jar. The activities allow students to draw upon several strands of mathematics as they apply new knowledge and skills to assist them in an estimation contest. Mathematical topics covered in this guided investigation include estimation by partitioning, by volume, by mass, and by sampling; computation mentally, by pencil and paper, and by calculator; fractional parts; liquid measurement; weight measurement; and multiple means of problem solving.

Set up an area in the room to display the contest materials. We recommend using a clear, unbreakable container such as a plastic peanut butter jar to hold the pennies. The label need not be removed, for it may provide useful clues that will help students refine their estimates. The teacher will need to provide the display, the jars (2), 2 envelopes, pennies for the contest (about $25 worth), paper penny rollers (request them from the bank when acquiring the pennies), and contest prizes, if desired.

Have the display prepared for students the day they begin the unit. Each student will have two estimates considered in the contest. Their first estimate may be little better than a guess. The activities throughout the unit should enable students to improve their initial estimates. Their last estimates may be close to the actual count if they exercise care in the investigations.

During this unit, students will employ multiple means of refining their estimates of the number of pennies in a jar. It is suggested that the display area be accessible to students throughout the unit for independent investigation.

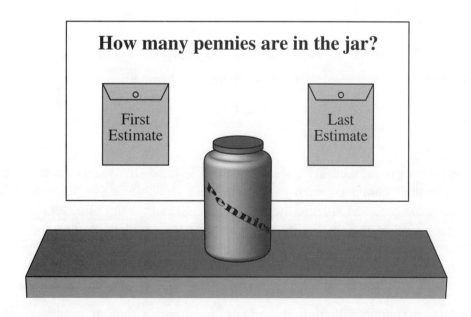

Activity 30   **Penny Jar–First Estimate**

Review

daily almanac activities

mental math

- Count by 9's from 9 to 99.

- Count by 10's from 5 to 105.

- Count by 50's from 50 to 500.

- How many yards is a mile? How many feet is a mile?

- How many days are in four weeks? Five weeks? Six weeks?

- Tanya paid a dollar for an item that cost 83¢. How much money should Tanya get back? What coins should she get back?   *17¢; 1 dime, 1 nickel, 2 pennies*

- On your U.S. map, how many inches is it from Kansas City to Los Angeles? About how many miles is that?   *$3\frac{1}{2}$ in.; 1400 mi*

- Count by fourths from $\frac{1}{2}$ to $2\frac{1}{2}$.

problem solving

- Simpson is a town between Ashlan and Winter Creek. From Simpson to Ashlan is 26 miles. From Simpson to Winter Creek is 42 miles. How far is it from Ashlan to Winter Creek?   *68 miles*

Materials Needed

- Contest display, including unbreakable jar filled with pennies

- A slip of paper for each student to make his or her first estimate

- A copy of "Penny Jar Activity Sheet" (Master 12) for each student

Activity

Distribute a copy of "Penny Jar Activity Sheet" (Master 12) and a small slip of paper to each student. Have students write their names on each paper. Then ask the children to guess to themselves the number of pennies in the jar and to record their guesses on the small slip of paper and in the first box of the activity sheet. Collect the small slips of paper with the students' names and estimates. (The students retain the larger activity sheet.) Store the slips in the "First Estimate" envelope on the display board and seal the envelope. The envelope will be opened and winners determined at the end of the unit.

Ask volunteers to announce their first estimate and explain their reasoning. Considering the opinions and reasonings of others is an indirect way of refining an estimate. Following the discussion, allow students to revise their first estimate based upon the explanations they have heard.

Activity 31   **Penny Jar–Second Estimate**

Review

daily almanac activities

mental math

- Count by 12's from 12 to 84.

- Count by 50's from 50 to 500.

- How many inches is four feet? Five feet? Ten feet?

- How many feet are in one yard? Two yards? Three yards? Ten yards?

- From the 2nd to the 25th is how many weeks and days?   *3 weeks, 2 days*

- On your U.S. map, how many inches is it from Chicago to Los Angeles? About how many miles is that? $4\frac{1}{4}$ *in.; 1700 mi*

- Count by fourths from $\frac{1}{4}$ to $2\frac{1}{4}$.

problem solving

- What month is halfway between September and May?   *January*

Materials Needed

- An empty jar of the same size and shape as the penny jar (will also be needed for Activity 32)

- A small paper cup or other small container (Save this container for Activity 32.)

- About 300 rolled pennies (6 rolls)

Activity

As students watch, the teacher or a selected student opens and empties rolls of pennies into a small paper cup or other small container until it is filled. Students should count along as the rolls are emptied. When the small cup is filled and the count is known by all, transfer the coins from the cup to the empty jar. Pass the partially filled jar around the room so that students can determine the approximate portion of the container that has been filled by the cup of pennies. Encourage students to discuss how many cups of pennies would be needed to fill the container. Then ask students to make their second estimate of the number of pennies in the penny jar and to record their estimates on the activity sheet for Day 2.

Note: When time allows, have volunteers re-roll the pennies used in this activity. The re-rolled pennies will be needed for Activity 33.

Activity 32 — Penny Jar–Third Estimate

Review

daily almanac activities

mental math

- Count by 7's from 7 to 84.

- How many days is five weeks? Six weeks? Seven weeks?

- Count by 3's from 3 to 36.

- How many feet are in three yards? Four yards? Five yards?

- Count by 50's from 50 to 500.

- How many pennies are in one roll? Two rolls? Four rolls?

- On your U.S. map, how many inches is it from Denver to Washington, D.C.? About how many miles is that?   *3 ¾ in.; 1500 mi*

problem solving

- From Goldrock to Willow through Hampton is 67 miles. If the distance from Hampton to Willow is 36 miles, how far is it from Goldrock to Willow?   *31 mi*

Material Needed

- An empty jar of the same size and shape as the penny jar

- The same small paper cup or other container used in Activity 31

- An adequate supply of water (or dry rice or beans) to fill the empty jar

Activity

As students watch, fill the small paper cup or container used in Activity 31 with water (or dry alternative) and then transfer the contents into the empty jar. Repeat the procedure as students count until the jar is full. You may choose to allow students to conduct this activity themselves. This activity coupled with the Day 2 activity should provide students with enough information to further refine their estimate.

Ask students to make their third estimate of the number of pennies in the jar and to record their estimates on the activity sheet for Day 3.

Activity 33   **Penny Jar–Fourth Estimate**

Review

daily almanac activities

mental math
- Count by 9's from 9 to 108.
- Count by 10's from 7 to 107.
- At what temperatures does water freeze and boil in the Fahrenheit and Celsius systems?
- How many inches is three feet? Four feet? Five feet? Six feet?
- Count by 50's from 50 to 600.
- How many pennies are in one roll? Two rolls? Three rolls? Ten rolls?
- Count by fourths from $\frac{1}{4}$ to $2\frac{1}{4}$.

problem solving
- What time is halfway between 8:00 a.m. and 3:00 p.m.?   *11:30 a.m.*

Materials Needed
- About 600 pennies in rolls

Activity

This activity may be explained to the entire class at one time. However, the actual physical activity may need to be performed individually or in small groups as time allows during the day. It is suggested that the rolls of pennies be available near the penny jar display during this activity.

Provide about 12 well-wrapped rolls of pennies for students to use to physically compare the perceived volume and weight of a known quantity of pennies to the volume and weight of the penny jar.

With the wrapped penny rolls, students can use their physical senses and reasoning to determine how many *rolls* of pennies, and from that how many *pennies*, would be needed to fill the penny jar. Students record their estimate on the activity sheet for Day 4.

Looking ahead: Activity 34 will ask students to compare the actual weight of two rolls of pennies with the weight of the penny jar. Materials needed for this activity include a scale and calculators for computation. If scales are not available at the school site, the teacher may want to find another means of weighing the pennies (e.g., using postal scales) prior to Activity 34.

Activity 34   **Penny Jar–Fifth Estimate**

Review

daily almanac activities

mental math

- Count by 12's from 12 to 96.

- How many months is two years? Three years? Ten years?

- Count by 3's from 3 to 36.

- How many feet is two yards? Five yards? Ten yards?

- Count by quarters from 25¢ to $2.00.

- Count by fourths from $\frac{1}{4}$ to 2.

- On your U.S. map, how many inches is it from Atlanta to Salt Lake City? About how many miles is that?   *$3\frac{3}{4}$ in.; 1500 mi*

problem solving

- From 8 p.m. to 7 a.m. is how many hours?   *11 hr*

- What time is halfway between 8 p.m. and 7 a.m?   *1:30 a.m.*

Materials Needed

- Scales or other means of determining the weight or mass of 2 rolls of pennies (100 pennies) and of the filled penny jar

- Calculators for computation

- Slips of paper for submitting final estimates

Activity

If the tools for performing this activity are not available, omit this activity and simply have students make their final best estimate of the number of pennies in the jar based upon their investigation. The final estimates should be recorded for Day 5 on the activity sheet and on small slips of paper with the students' names. Collect the slips of paper and store them in the "Final Estimate" envelope of the display. Students should keep the activity sheet until the end of the unit.

Step 1: Determine the weight (or mass) of two rolls of pennies (100 pennies) and of the filled penny jar. Both measurements should be in the same units (e.g., ounces-ounces or grams-grams).

Step 2: Use a calculator to find the number of hundreds of pennies required to equal the weight of the filled penny jar by dividing the weight of the jar by the weight of the two rolls of pennies.

Step 3: Make sense of the answer. The whole-number portion of the answer (to the left of the decimal point in the display) represents the number of hundreds of pennies. For instance, if the display reads 15.875, then the weight of the penny jar is somewhat more than 15 times the weight of 100 pennies. Thus, there might be fifteen hundred to sixteen hundred (1500–1600) pennies in the jar.

Step 4: Evaluate the calculation in light of the other activities in the unit. This activity does not necessarily produce the most accurate results. Inaccuracies in measuring the weights and discounting the weight of the container affect the accuracy of the results. However, this calculation, considered with previous calculations, should help students make a final estimate of the number of pennies in the jar. Have students record a final best estimate on the activity sheet and on slips of paper with their names. Collect the final estimates and store them in the envelope at the display area. In the next activity students will count and roll the pennies.

Activity 35 **Penny Count**

Review

daily almanac activities

mental math

- Count by 7's from 7 to 84.

- How many days is three weeks? Five weeks? Ten weeks?

- Count by 12's from 12 to 96.

- How many inches is three feet? Five feet? Six feet?

- Count by 10's from 8 to 108.

- Natalie paid a dollar for an item that cost 54¢. How much money should she get back? What coins should she get back? *46¢; 1 quarter, 2 dimes, 1 penny*

problem solving

- How many days are there from April 3 to May 17? *44 days*

- How many days are there from May 3 to June 17? *45 days*

Materials Needed

- Empty penny rollers for the pennies in the jar

- Contest prizes, if desired

Activity

In this activity, students will count and roll the pennies from the penny jar and complete their activity sheet. Then they will consider the first and final estimates to determine contest winners.

Counting pennies: Have students work in pairs to count and roll the pennies from the penny jar. Distribute two empty penny rollers per pair of students. Unseal the penny jar and deposit a small handful of pennies with each pair of students. Each student should immediately begin counting out 50 pennies for their penny roll and set any excess pennies aside. After emptying the penny jar, gather these excess pennies for any students who did not receive pennies from the jar. Students should check each other's count and then put the pennies neatly into a penny roller. Comparing the lengths of the rolls of pennies serves as an additional check. Rolling coins requires some dexterity. Students may need some guidance to successfully complete this task.

When all the pennies are rolled or accounted for, have the class count the rolls and any excess coins to determine the number of pennies that were in the jar. Have students suggest counting strategies (e.g., counting rolls (50's) or counting pairs of rolls (100's)). When the final count has been agreed upon and posted, have students complete their activity sheets before opening the contest envelopes.

Determining winners: Unseal the "First Estimate" envelope and gather the estimates. Read estimates (not names) and sort by class response: "close" or "not close." Re-sort by class response, if necessary, until five or six estimates remain for closer evaluation. Post these remaining numbers near the posted penny count and allow time for the class to determine the closest estimate. Solicit explanations from volunteers for how they decided which was closest. When the winning estimate has been determined, repeat the process with the estimates from the second envelope.

Extensions: If class enthusiasm for these activities has been evident, additional estimation investigations may be planned. Consider re-using the display materials to estimate the number of beans, teddy bear counters, or other items in the jar. Students might work individually or in teams. They could plan their own investigations and conduct their own experiments to assist their estimation.

UNIT 5   DOUBLES AND HALVES

"Doubles and Halves" is a unit that provides introductory activities in topics that are rich in mathematics, including exponential growth and decay, discrete mathematics, probability, geometry, measurement, and number theory.

Activity 36   Double Your Money

Review

daily almanac activities

mental math

- Count by 7's from 7 to 84.
- Count by 10's from 6 to 106.
- Count by 50's from 50 to 500.
- How many yards is a mile? How many feet is a mile? *1760 yards; 5280 feet*
- Leonard paid a dollar for an item that cost 23¢. How much money should he get back? What coins should he get back? *77¢; 3 quarters, 2 pennies*
- On your U.S. map, how many inches is it from San Francisco to New York City? About how many miles is that? *$6\frac{1}{2}$ in.; 2600 mi*
- Count by fourths from $1\frac{3}{4}$ to $3\frac{1}{2}$.

Materials Needed

- A copy of "Double Your Money Table" (Master 13) for each student

Problem-Solving Activity: Complete a Table

Prepare to distribute copies of Master 13 after reading the following story. It is suggested that students work in pairs or in small groups to complete the table.

   "Completing a table makes some problems easier to solve. A table is a way to organize your thinking, to keep track of numbers, and to help you see patterns. Listen to this story about doubling. After the story, you will complete a table to help you answer the questions at the end of the story."

"Doubling something makes it twice as big. If you double a recipe, it makes twice as much food. If you double a dollar, it makes two dollars. Here is a story about doubling. Read the story carefully. Then figure out the answer to the question at the end."

James and John were asked to take care of their neighbor's house while the neighbor was on vacation for twelve days. For taking in the mail, watering the plants, and feeding the cat, John asked to be paid $1.00 each day. James asked for only 1¢ the first day, 2¢ the second day, 4¢ the third day, and so on. The neighbor agreed to pay John a dollar each day and to double the amount James would be paid each day. Then the neighbor went on vacation. The boys did their jobs each day and kept track of how much they had earned on a table like this one. (Show table.) When the neighbor returned, the boys were paid. How much did each boy receive?

Distribute a copy of Master 13 to each student and monitor students' work.

MASTER 13 **DOUBLE YOUR MONEY TABLE**

	John's Pay		James' Pay	
	Day's Pay	Total Pay	Day's Pay	Total Pay
Day 1	$1	$1	1¢	1¢
Day 2	$1	$2	2¢	3¢
Day 3	$1	$3	4¢	7¢
Day 4	$1	$4	8¢	15¢
Day 5	$1	$5	16¢	31¢
Day 6	$1	$6	32¢	63¢
Day 7	$1	$7	64¢	$1.27
Day 8	$1	$8	$1.28	$2.55
Day 9	$1	$9	$2.56	$5.11
Day 10	$1	$10	$5.12	$10.23
Day 11	$1	$11	$10.24	$20.47
Day 12	$1	$12	$20.48	$40.95

1. How much had each boy earned after 6 days?

   John had earned $6, and James had earned 63¢.

2. After which day were the boys' totals about the same?

   After Day 10, John had earned $10, and James had earned $10.23.

3. How much was each boy paid?

   John was paid $12. James was paid $40.95.

4. What pattern can you find in the last two columns of the chart?

   Various patterns could be described. The amount in the last column is one cent less than twice the amount in the same row of the third column.

Name_____

Activity 37   **Double Trees**

Review

daily almanac activities

mental math

- Double each of these numbers: 5, 6, 7, 10.   *10, 12, 14, 20*

- Find half of each of these numbers: 10, 50, 100.   *5, 25, 50*

- If you double 1, the answer is 2. If you double 2, the answer is 4. Keep doubling until the answer is 32.   *8, 16, 32*

- Half of 16 is 8. Half of 8 is 4. Keep finding halves until the answer is $\frac{1}{2}$.   *2, 1, $\frac{1}{2}$*

- A mile is how many yards? How many feet?   *1760 yards; 5280 feet*

problem solving

- What month is halfway between July and May?   *December*

Materials Needed

- A copy of "Double Trees" (Master 14) for each student or pair of students

Activity

A "double tree" is a design in which each branch divides into two branches. Double trees can be used to make a family tree or to keep track of games in a tournament.

Sketch the following outline of a family tree on the board for the class to see:

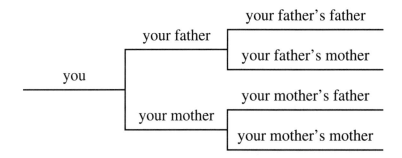

Then distribute the activity sheet "Double Trees" (Master 14). Have students compare the family tree on the activity sheet with the outline of a family tree on the board. Ask students to answer the questions on the activity sheet below the family tree.

As an extension, consider having students sketch a similar family tree for themselves.

Double trees (commonly called "tournament ladders") are used to keep track of matches and winners in tournaments. The activity sheet shows the results of a table tennis tournament among four players. In the first round, Ted defeated Bob and Alice defeated Carol. Then Ted and Alice played each other and Alice won. After discussing the tournament ladder, have students answer the questions below the ladder.

As an extension, have students develop a tournament ladder for an eight-player tournament.

MASTER 14   **DOUBLE TREES**

This diagram shows part of Holly's family tree.

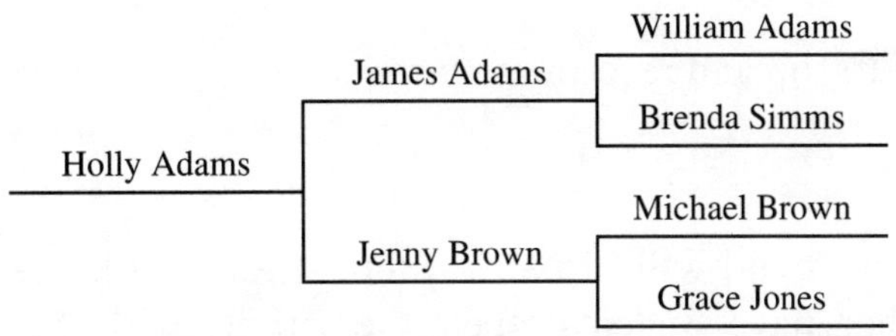

Holly Adams — James Adams — William Adams / Brenda Simms; Jenny Brown — Michael Brown / Grace Jones

Who is Holly's grandfather on her mother's side? _____ Michael Brown _____

What is Holly's father's mother's maiden name? _____ Brenda Simms _____

This diagram shows the games and winners in a table tennis tournament.

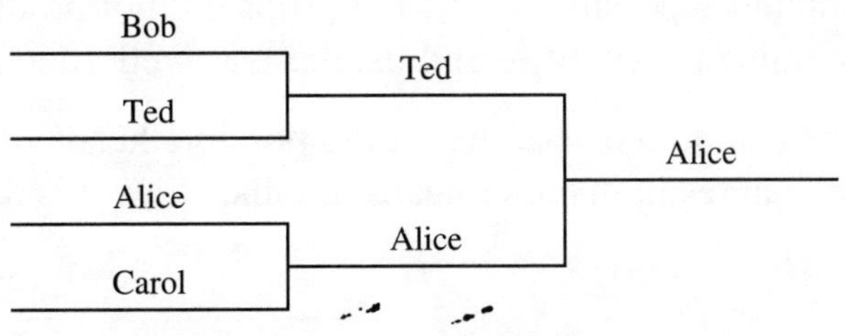

Bob / Ted → Ted; Alice / Carol → Alice; Ted vs Alice → Alice

Who played Carol in the first match? _____ Alice _____

Who was the loser in the championship game? _____ Ted _____

Activity 38   **Heads or Tails**

Review

daily almanac activities

mental math

- If you double 1, the answer is 2. If you double 2, the answer is 4. Keep doubling until the answer is 64.

- Half of 8 is 4. Half of 4 is 2. Keep finding halves until the answer is $\frac{1}{4}$.

Materials Needed

- Each group needs a coin to flip and recording materials.

Activity

Have students work in pairs. One child will flip a coin three times while the other child records the results on a piece of paper. Then have students repeat the activity with the roles reversed. Ask the students to follow these directions:

> *"Flip a coin. On a piece of paper write 'H' if the coin lands heads up or 'T' if the coin lands tails up. Flip the coin again and write 'H' or 'T' after the first letter. Then flip the coin a third time and write 'H' or 'T' after the second letter. When you finish, you should have three letters on your paper, such as HTT."*

Allow time for students to complete the coin flips and record the results. Then post the results as follows: Ask volunteers to read their letter combinations while the teacher or a designated student records the letter combinations in a column for all to see. Continue to solicit different arrangements of letters.

There are eight different outcomes possible. If the coin flips did not produce all eight outcomes, ask students to imagine the remaining possibilities and list these as well. (See list below.)

Announce that a double tree can help determine all the possible heads or tails outcomes from a series of coin flips. The first flip can result in either heads or tails. Draw this diagram on your paper:

If the first flip is heads, then the second flip could be heads or tails. Extend your diagram like this:

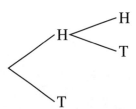

If the first flip is tails, then the second flip could still be heads or tails. Finish your two-flip diagram.

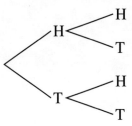

Using this diagram, we can see that with two flips of a coin there are four possible outcomes: HH, HT, TH, or TT.

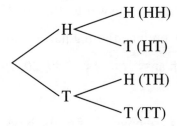

Now we will show one more coin flip for each of these possibilities. Complete this diagram:

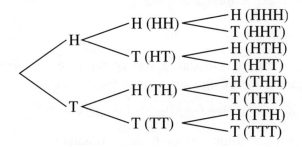

Compare the double tree list of outcomes with the previous list and resolve any discrepancies. Then count the number of students whose coin flips resulted in each outcome and post these numbers next to each outcome. Were all outcomes produced by student coin flips?

Sketch this table on the chalkboard and ask students to state the number of possible outcomes of 1, 2, and 3 coin flips. Then ask students to predict the number of possible outcomes of 4 coin flips. Some students should notice that the number of outcomes doubles with each additional flip of the coin. The number of possible outcomes of 4 coin flips is 16.

Extension: Ask students to make a double tree for 4 coin flips and to list the possible outcomes.

Activity 39   **U.S. Liquid Measure**

Review

daily almanac activities

mental math

- If you double 1, the answer is 2. If you double 2, the answer is 4. Continue doubling until the answer is 128.   *8, 16, 32, 64, 128*

- Double 3 and continue doubling each answer to 48.   *6, 12, 24, 48*

- Half of 16 is 8. Half of 8 is 4. Continue finding halves until the answer is $\frac{1}{8}$.

- Find half of 80 and half of each answer to $2\frac{1}{2}$.   *40, 20, 10, 5, $2\frac{1}{2}$*

problem solving

- Half of the students in the class are boys. Half of the boys walk to school. Half of the boys who walk to school carry their lunches. If four boys walk to school carrying their lunches, then how many students are in the class?   *32*

Materials Needed

- The following five containers: measuring cup or 8-ounce container, one pint container, one quart container, half-gallon container, one gallon container

- Water or dry substitute such as rice for filling containers

- A funnel may be helpful for filling narrow-necked containers.

Activity

Display all five containers on a desk or table.

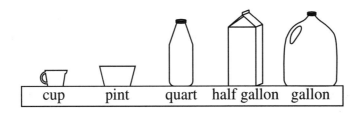

First ask students to predict the number of cups of water that would be needed to fill a pint container, the number of pints of water that would be needed to fill a quart container, and so on. Then conduct the activity by filling (or having a selected student fill) …

>   the pint container, using the cup container twice,

>   the quart container, using the pint container twice,

>   the half-gallon container, using the quart container twice, and

>   the gallon container, using the half-gallon container twice.

Ask the following questions:

"How many cups are in a pint? A quart? A half-gallon? A gallon?"   *2; 4; 8; 16*

"How many pints are in a quart? A half-gallon? A gallon?"   *2; 4; 8*

"How many quarts are in a half-gallon? A gallon?"   *2; 4*

"How many quarters are in a dollar?"   *4*

"Why is a 25-cent piece called a quarter?"   *A quarter is a fourth. A quarter is one fourth of a dollar.*

"Why is a quart called a quart?"   *A quart is one fourth of a gallon.*

Activity 40   **Eighths of an Inch**

Review

daily almanac activities

mental math

- Double 1 and continue doubling each answer to 128.   *2, 4, 8, 16, 32, 64, 128*

- Double 5 and continue doubling each answer to 160.   *10, 20, 40, 80, 160*

- Find half of 8 and half of each consecutive answer to $\frac{1}{8}$.   *4, 2, 1, $\frac{1}{2}$, $\frac{1}{4}$, $\frac{1}{8}$*

- Find half of 24 and half of each consecutive answer to $1\frac{1}{2}$.   *12, 6, 3, $1\frac{1}{2}$*

- On the U.S. map, how many inches is it from Boston to Dallas? About how many miles is that?   *$3\frac{3}{4}$ in.; 1500 mi*

problem solving

- Mark is in class for half of half of a day. How many hours is Mark in class?   *6 hr*

Materials Needed

- A copy of "Measuring to the Nearest Eighth Inch" (Master 15) for each student

- Each student needs his or her tagboard ruler from Activity 24.

- Optional: The entire ruler may be re-marked using a new strip of construction paper.

Activity

"In an earlier activity you made an inch ruler out of tagboard. You divided the ruler into quarters of an inch. In this activity you will divide the ruler into eighths of an inch. First we will review how we marked the quarter-inch ruler."

"First you made marks on a strip of tagboard one inch apart. Next, you divided the distance in half by making half-inch marks. That made the distance between marks $\frac{1}{2}$ of an inch. Then you divided that distance in half by making quarter-inch marks. That made the distance between marks $\frac{1}{4}$ of an inch. Each new set of marks you drew was shorter."

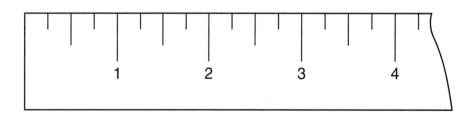

*"Now you will divide the distance between the marks in half again. This will divide the ruler into **eighths** of an inch. Make the marks shorter than the quarter-inch marks. When you are finished, your ruler should look like this."*

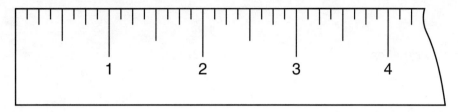

"Now the distance between marks is $\frac{1}{8}$ of an inch."

Count on the ruler by eighths of an inch: $\frac{1}{8}$, $\frac{2}{8} = \frac{1}{4}$, $\frac{3}{8}$, $\frac{4}{8} = \frac{1}{2}$, $\frac{5}{8}$, $\frac{6}{8} = \frac{3}{4}$, $\frac{7}{8}$, $\frac{8}{8} = 1$, $1\frac{1}{8}$, $1\frac{2}{8} = 1\frac{1}{4}$, ...

Distribute Master 15 and have students measure the segments and figures on the activity sheet.

MASTER 15   **MEASURING TO THE NEAREST EIGHTH INCH**

Find the length of each line segment.

1. ————————————   The length is ___$2\frac{1}{8}$ in.___.

2. ————————————   The length is ___$2\frac{7}{8}$ in.___.

3. ——————————————   The length is ___$4\frac{5}{8}$ in.___.

Find the length and width of each rectangle.

4.   length ___$1\frac{3}{4}$ in.___   width ___$1\frac{3}{8}$ in.___

5.   length ___$2\frac{3}{8}$ in.___   width ___$\frac{7}{8}$ in.___

6. How long is this paper? ___11 in.___
   How wide is this paper? ___$8\frac{1}{2}$ in.___

Find the length of each object.

7. How long is your pencil? _____

8. How long is your little finger? _____

9. How long is your shoe? _____

10. Find an object to measure. Name the object and write its length.

   _____

Activity 41   **Halves of Even and Odd Numbers**

Review

daily almanac activities

mental math
- Count by eighths from $\frac{1}{8}$ to 1.
- Count by 3's from 3 to 36.
- How many feet are in four yards? Five yards? Six yards?
- Count by 7's to 84.
- How many days are in five weeks? Six weeks? Seven weeks?
- On your U.S. map, how many inches is it from St. Louis to New York City? About how many miles is that?   *$2\frac{1}{4}$ in.; 900 mi*

problem solving
- Oak Grove is halfway between Chester and Glenwood. From Chester to Oak Grove is 24 miles. How far is the round trip from Chester to Glenwood and back to Chester?   *96 miles*

Materials Needed

- Money pouch with $100, $10, and $1 bills; and 10 dimes or facsimiles for each pair of students
- A copy of "Dividing Money in Half" (Master 16) for each pair of students

Activity

Distribute Master 16 and guide the class through the first two exercises before allowing pairs of students to work on their own.

First exercise: "Finding Half of $356"

Have students place three $100 bills, five $10 bills, and six $1 bills on their desks.

"Is $356 an even or odd number of dollars? How can we tell?"

> *It is an even number of dollars. We can tell by counting the number of ones. An even number of ones means that the entire number is even.*

"Write the word 'even' on your activity sheet in the box to the right of $356."

"Now we will divide the bills in half. We will make two equal groups of money. We will put the money in the two boxes on the activity sheet. First we will divide the $100 bills. We do not tear it in half. Instead, we trade the extra $100 bill to the bank for ten $10 bills. Make the trade."

"Now we have a total of fifteen $10 bills to divide in half. We put seven $10 bills in each box …. We still have a $10 bill. We trade the $10 bill to the bank for ten $1 bills."

"Now we have sixteen $1 bills. Half of sixteen is eight. We put eight $1 bills in each box. Now we count the money to be sure the amount in each box is the same. Each box should contain half of $356."

"How much is half of $356?"   *$178*

"Write $178 on your activity sheet for half of $356."

"Now clear the money from your activity sheet and we will do the next exercise."

Second exercise: **"Finding Half of $365"**

Have students place three $100 bills, six $10 bills, and five $1 bills on their desks.

"Is $365 an even or odd number of dollars?"   *odd number*

"Write the word 'odd' on your activity sheet."

"First divide the three $100 bills in half. Exchange with the bank, if necessary."

"Next, divide all the $10 bills in half. Is it necessary to exchange a $10 bill with the bank?"   *no*

"Now we divide the five $1 bills in half. We put two $1 bills in each box. We still have a $1 bill. Instead of tearing the $1 bill in half, we trade it for ten dimes. Make the trade."

"We put half of the ten dimes in each box."

"Count the money in each box. How much is half of $365?"   *$182.50*

"Instead of saying '$182.50,' we could say '182$\frac{1}{2}$' dollars."

"Why do you suppose we ended up with half dollars in each box this time?" *Look for answers that note that the starting amount was an odd number.*

Have students work on exercises 3 and 4 with a partner. For exercises 5 and 6, students invent their own number to divide in half. For exercise 5 they should select an even number; for exercise 6 they should select an odd number.

Activity 42

Calculator Activity: Halves of Evens and Odds

Review

daily almanac activities

mental math

- Count by eighths from $\frac{1}{8}$ to $1\frac{1}{2}$.

- Count by 9's from 9 to 99.

- Count by 10's from 9 to 99.

- How many days are there in January, February, and March in a common year?

- Start with $\frac{1}{4}$ and begin doubling until the answer is 64.

problem solving

- One school had 62 students in one grade. The students were divided as evenly as possible into two classrooms. How many students were in each classroom?   *31 students*

- Another school had 61 students in one grade. Again the students were divided as evenly as possible into two classrooms. How many students were in each classroom?   *There were 30 students in one classroom and 31 students in the other classroom. Some things cannot be divided in half.*

Materials Needed

- A calculator for each pair of students

- A copy of the "Calculator Activity Recording Sheet" (Master 17) for each pair of students

Activity

Review with students that an identifying characteristic of even numbers is that the digit in the ones' place is a 0, 2, 4, 6, or 8.

Arrange students in pairs and distribute a calculator and a recording sheet (Master 17) to each pair of students. One student should enter a number into the calculator and on the recording sheet. Students should then agree whether the entered number is even or odd and record their decision on the sheet. The second student should press [÷] [2] [=] to find half of the entered number, which is then written on the recording sheet. Then the second student clears the calculator, enters a number, and the activity is repeated. Have each student enter two even and two odd numbers. Students should then complete the remaining parts of the activity sheet.

MASTER 17   # CALCULATOR ACTIVITY RECORDING SHEET

Number Entered	Even or Odd	Half of Number
37,254	even	18,627
1.		
2.		
3.		
4.		
5.		
6.		
7.		
8.		

Look for a pattern in this table. On the lines below, describe any pattern that you see.

Half of an even number is a whole number.

Half of an odd number is not a whole number. Half of an odd number ends with $\frac{1}{2}$ or .5.

Read this story; then answer the questions.

Mark entered a number into a calculator and then divided by two. The calculator's display showed 1324.5.

a. Was the original number Mark entered even or odd? odd

b. How could you find the number Mark entered? To find the number Mark entered, enter 1324.5 and multiply by 2.

c. Which number is larger, 1324.5 or $1324\frac{1}{2}$? They are equal.

Name_____   Name_____

Activity 43   **Symmetrical Cut-Outs**

Review

almanac activities

mental math

- Count by eighths from 1 to 2.

- Count by 12's from 12 to 96.

- How many inches are in three feet? Five feet? Six feet?   *36 in.; 60 in.; 72 in.*

- How many inches are in half of half a foot?   *3 in.*

- How many cents are in half of half a dollar?   *25¢*

problem solving

- On Monday, Simon walked a quarter mile. On Tuesday, Simon walked twice as far as he walked on Monday. On Wednesday, Simon walked twice as far as he did on Tuesday. How many yards did Simon walk on Wednesday?   *1760 yards*

Materials Needed

- Two sheets of unlined paper for each student

- Scissors

Activity

*Explain to the class that a **line of symmetry** divides a figure in half so that the halves are mirror images. A line of symmetry also shows where a plane figure could be "folded in half" so that one half exactly fits on the other half.*

Demonstration 1:   Fold a sheet of paper in half. While the paper is folded, cut a shape from the paper. Start the cut from the folded edge and end the cut with the folded edge, as shown.

The opened figure has a line of symmetry along the fold.

Student Activity 1:   Ask the students to fold a sheet of paper once and to cut a shape from the sheet, starting and ending the cut at the folded edge. Have volunteers show their symmetric cut-outs and identify the line of symmetry.

Demonstration 2:   Explain that a figure may have more than one line of symmetry. Fold a sheet of paper in half, and then fold the folded sheet in half, as shown.

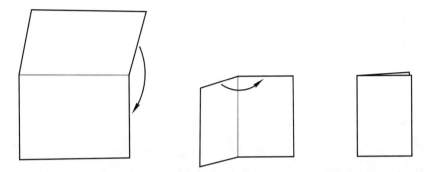

Cut a shape from the twice-folded paper, beginning the cut from one folded edge and ending the cut at the other folded edge.

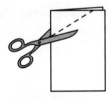

The opened figure has two lines of symmetry along the folds.

Student Activity 2:   Ask students to fold a sheet of paper twice and to cut a shape from one folded edge to the other folded edge. Before they open it, ask them to imagine what the shape will look like. Have volunteers show their cut-outs.

Activity 44   Finding Lines of Symmetry

Review

daily almanac activities

mental math

- Count by eighths from $\frac{1}{8}$ to 2.
- Count by 7's from 7 to 84.
- Start with $\frac{1}{8}$ and begin doubling to 64.
- Start with 48 and begin dividing in half to $1\frac{1}{2}$.
- How many inches is $\frac{1}{2}$ foot? $1\frac{1}{2}$ feet?   *6 in.; 18 in.*
- How many hours are in $\frac{1}{2}$ day? $1\frac{1}{2}$ days?   *12 hr; 36 hr*

problem solving

- Larry said, "I want half of the money." Moe said, "I'll give you half of half the money." Curly said, "I want half of what Larry gets." If Curly got $5, how much money did Larry get and how much was left for Moe?   *Larry got $10, and $25 was left for Moe.*

Materials Needed

- A copy of the "Lines of Symmetry Activity Sheet" (Master 18) for each student
- A safety mirror for each student or pair of students is a helpful, but optional, manipulative.

Activity

Review with the class that a line of symmetry divides a figure in half so that the halves are mirror images. Some figures have two lines of symmetry, some have more than two lines of symmetry, and some figures have no lines of symmetry.

Distribute a "Lines of Symmetry Activity Sheet" (Master 18) to each student. Students will sketch the lines of symmetry, if any, for each figure.

If safety mirrors are available, have students participate in the following optional activity. If safety mirrors are not available, students will need to imagine where a figure could be folded upon itself.

Optional activity: Distribute a safety mirror to each student or small group of students. Explain that a mirror can help to locate lines of symmetry. An upright mirror placed on a line of symmetry will visually recreate the entire figure.

     Have students slide the edge of a mirror across a figure on the activity sheet so that they can see the reflection. When the edge of the mirror is placed on a line of symmetry, the entire figure should be "visible." The line(s) of symmetry should be sketched on figures that have a line of symmetry.

MASTER 18

LINES OF SYMMETRY
ACTIVITY SHEET

Draw one line of symmetry for each figure:

1.    2. 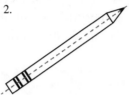   3.

Draw two lines of symmetry for each figure:

4. 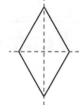   5. 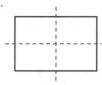   6.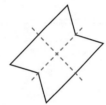

Draw one, two, or more lines of symmetry for each figure.
One figure has no lines of symmetry.

 one

 two

four

 one

no lines of symmetry

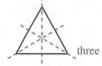 three

Describe what a line of symmetry is. Then draw a figure on the back of this paper that has a line of symmetry.

_____

_____

_____

UNIT 6   GRIDS

The activities within this unit cover the mathematical topics of area, perimeter, enlargement, and first-quadrant rectangular coordinates. Masters 19–22 are used in these activities. Floor tiles may be used to physically represent units of area, while toothpicks may represent units of length. When students are asked to find the area of a shape, encourage them to count squares. When they are asked to find a perimeter, suggest that they count the number of small segments (i.e., toothpicks) around the shape. The pairs of numbers on Master 22 are coordinates. The two numbers provide the "address" of a point on the grid. Starting from the lower left corner of the grid, the numbers indicate first how far to the right and then how far up to move to locate the point. Some students remember the order as "First walk; then climb."

Activity 45   Square Feet

Review

daily almanac activities

mental math

- Sam bought a notebook for $2.98 and a pad of paper for $1.98. About how much did Sam pay for the notebook and paper?   *About $5 (Exactly $4.96 plus tax)*

- Sarah paid a dollar for an item that cost 46¢. How much money should Sarah get back? What coins should she get back?   *54¢; 2 quarters and 4 pennies*

- How many days are in the first six months of a common year?

- Double 1 cup and continue doubling to 1 gallon.   *Pint, quart, half gallon, gallon*

problem solving

- Write the first five letters of the alphabet as capitals. Then draw a line of symmetry for each letter. What is the next capital letter of the alphabet that has exactly one line of symmetry?   *The letters H and I each have two lines of symmetry. The next letter with one line of symmetry is M. (Note: Lines of symmetry may vary depending on individual handwriting.)*

Materials Needed

- Three pieces of construction paper cut into 12" × 12" squares for each student (*Note*: After the activity, collect and save intact squares for Activity 46.)

- A pair of scissors for each group

Introduction

Students will use the construction paper squares to find the approximate area of a desktop and of a tabletop. A bulletin board or a room or cabinet door may substitute for a table if necessary. These measures are approximations. Students should primarily use entire squares. Discourage unnecessary cutting of the construction paper squares.

"Your desktop has a surface that you can work on. A table has a surface on which we can spread books or papers or dishes. The classroom floor has a surface that supports desks and tables and cabinets. Each of these surfaces has an area. The area of a tabletop is greater than the area of a desktop. The area of the floor is greater than the area of a tabletop. Bulletin boards have an area, and walls have an area."

"To measure area, we imagine covering the surface with squares of a certain size. Today we will cover surfaces with square feet. This construction paper square covers an area of one square foot."

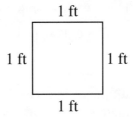

"If this square is cut into pieces, then all of the pieces together cover an area of one square foot."

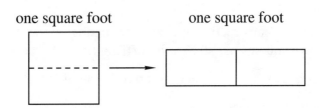

"You will use these construction paper squares to find the approximate area of a desktop and of a tabletop (or of a bulletin board or door if a table is not available).

Activity

Working in small groups, have students determine the fewest number of 1-foot squares needed to cover the top of a student desk. Students may cut a square and use the pieces.

Before clearing the desktop, have the group draw a picture showing how the squares and pieces fit on the desktop. Students should calculate the number of squares used and record the area of the desktop to the nearest square foot.

If desks are uniform, each group should find the desktops to have the same area even if they arrange the squares differently. Discuss differences.

Repeat the activity on a larger surface such as a tabletop, bulletin board, or door. The group may have an insufficient number of squares to cover the surface. However, the students should still be able to calculate the total number of squares needed to cover the surface. Again have each group draw a picture showing how the surface could be covered. Have groups report their results and their procedures.

Activity 46   **Floor Area**

Review

daily almanac activities

mental math

- Count by 12's from 12 to 96.

- How many inches are in four feet? Five feet? Five and one half feet?

- At what temperatures does water freeze and boil on the Celsius and Fahrenheit scales?

- Point to the northeast, northwest, southeast, southwest.

- Nick's little sister is $2\frac{1}{2}$ years old. How many months old is Nick's sister?   *30 months*

- Find half of a gallon and continue finding halves to 1 cup. $\frac{1}{2}$ *gallon, quart, pint, cup*

problem solving

- Eric used $2\frac{1}{2}$ sheets of 1-foot square paper to cover his desk. There are 6 desks in Eric's row. How many sheets of 1-foot square paper would be needed to cover all of the desks in the row?   *15*

Materials Needed

- 1-foot square sheets of construction paper (simulating floor tiles) remaining from Activity 45 (One or two squares per student is sufficient.)

- A sheet of quarter-inch grid paper for each group (or copy of Master 19)

- An available calculator is optional.

Activity

Working in small groups, have students determine the number of tiles needed to cover the floor of the classroom. By counting and moving their squares along two walls, students should be able to determine the number of tiles in each row and the number of rows of tiles.

Each group should then outline the pattern on a sheet of grid paper. Then by counting, adding, or multiplying, students should calculate the area of the room in square feet. Discuss students' results and procedures.

Activity 47   **Estimating Areas**

Review

daily almanac activities

mental math

- Count by 7's from 7 to 84.

- How many days is six weeks? Eight weeks? Ten weeks?

- How many days are in a leap year? Does a leap year have an odd or even number of days? *366 days; even*

- Count by eighths from 2 to 3.

- Find half of 64 and continue finding halves of each answer to $\frac{1}{8}$.

problem solving

- One pound of peanut brittle cost $5.00 and one pound of taffy cost $6.00. Tammy bought a quarter pound of each. How can we figure out how much Tammy had to pay?   *A quarter is half of a half. Half of $5.00 is $2.50. Half of $2.50 is $1.25, the price of the peanut brittle. Half of $6.00 is $3.00. Half of $3.00 is $1.50, the price of the taffy. Altogether, the cost was $2.75 plus any tax.*

Materials

- A sheet of square-inch grid paper for each student (Master 20)

Activity

Distribute the square-inch grid paper. Review with the class that surfaces are measured by calculating the number of squares of a certain size that would be needed to cover the surface. Each square on the grid paper is one square inch. Students will use the grid paper to estimate the area of the sole of one of their shoes.

Have students place a shoe on the grid paper and trace around it. Positioning the shoe so that the straighter, outside portion of the shoe aligns with a line on the grid paper will make the area calculation easier. By counting the squares within the outline of the shoe, students can estimate the area of the sole of the shoe. There are two strategies for counting:

First strategy: Count all of the squares that are entirely within the outline. Shading these may be helpful. Then estimate the number of squares that could be formed from the remaining parts of squares that are within the outline.

Second strategy: Count all of the squares that are entirely within the outline, as before. Then count all of the squares that seem to have half of their area within the outline. Do not count any squares that have less than half of their area within the outline.

Activity 48 **Perimeter and Area of Rectangles**

Review

daily almanac activities

mental math

- Count by 6's from 6 to 72.

- How many eggs are in $1\frac{1}{2}$ dozen?

- Rachel went to the store with $8.94. She spent $5.20. How much money did she have left? *$3.74*

- Tom turned ten years old in October. In what month will Tom be ten and one half years old? *April*

- Count by eighths from $\frac{1}{8}$ to 1.

problem solving

- The problem for students to solve is to plan the arrangement of the four rectangles the students are asked to draw in today's activity. The four rectangles should fit on one side of the grid paper. Edges may touch, but the rectangles should not overlap.

Materials Needed

- A copy of square-inch grid paper per student (Master 20)

- A copy of the "Perimeter and Area of Rectangles" activity sheet (Master 21) for each student

- A wooden or plastic ruler for each student

Introduction

The distance around a shape is its *perimeter*. An "inch worm" named "Peri" may help students visualize perimeter. Peri the worm inches his way around rectangles and other polygons until he returns to the starting point. The total distance Peri travels is the perimeter of the figure. Around this rectangle Peri travels 4 inches, then 2 inches, then 4 inches, and then 2 inches, for a total of 12 inches.

The activity sheet asks students to draw four rectangles on square-inch grid paper. The rectangles named in the first column of the chart may be drawn by tracing over the lines of the grid paper. Students should plan the use of their grid paper so that all of the rectangles fit on one sheet. Some rectangles will share sides.

Looking ahead: Activity 49 asks students to make enlarged drawings. Students may want to bring illustrations from home that they would like to enlarge.

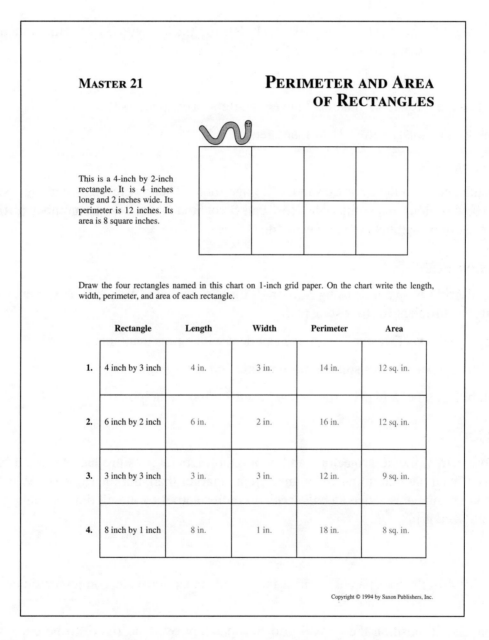

MASTER 21

PERIMETER AND AREA OF RECTANGLES

This is a 4-inch by 2-inch rectangle. It is 4 inches long and 2 inches wide. Its perimeter is 12 inches. Its area is 8 square inches.

Draw the four rectangles named in this chart on 1-inch grid paper. On the chart write the length, width, perimeter, and area of each rectangle.

	Rectangle	Length	Width	Perimeter	Area
1.	4 inch by 3 inch	4 in.	3 in.	14 in.	12 sq. in.
2.	6 inch by 2 inch	6 in.	2 in.	16 in.	12 sq. in.
3.	3 inch by 3 inch	3 in.	3 in.	12 in.	9 sq. in.
4.	8 inch by 1 inch	8 in.	1 in.	18 in.	8 sq. in.

Activity 49 **Enlargements**

Review

daily almanac activities

mental math

- Count by 25's from 25 to 300.

- James went to the theater with $10.00. He left the theater with $4.25. How much money did James spend at the theater?   *$5.75*

- Count by 5's from 1 to 41.   *1, 6, 11, 16, 21, 26, 31, 36, 41*

- How much money is six quarters? Seven quarters? Ten quarters?

- A mile is how many yards? How many feet?

problem solving

- Samantha counted the floor tiles in the storage room. There were 12 tiles along a side wall and 10 tiles along the front wall. How can Samantha figure out the number of tiles that cover the floor without counting each tile?

Materials Needed

- A small-grid transparency using Master 19 for each student (A single transparency cut into fourths is sufficient for four students.)

- A large-grid copy (Master 20) for each student with extras available

- Comics or other pictures suitable for drawing and enlarging

- Small bits of tape or paper clips for each student may be helpful.

Introduction

Overhead projectors, movie projectors, and photograph laboratories produce enlarged images using lenses. Lenses bend the light to make an image that is larger than, but the same shape as, the original image. The larger image is called an *enlargement*. In this activity you will draw an enlargement using two different-sized grids.

Activity

Distribute a small-grid transparency and a large-grid paper. Provide comics or other pictures for students who do not have their own.

Students should position their small-grid transparency over the figure to be copied. Taping or clipping the transparency in place may help to avoid shifting. Ask students to decide where they want to begin drawing. Beginning in the corresponding square on the large-grid paper, the student draws in the large-grid square the portion of the figure visible through the small grid. Moving from square to square, the drawing is continued until the figure is completed.

Extension: Students may create their own drawing grids to enlarge a figure to whatever size they wish. A student or group of students may use the technique to create a classroom mural.

Activity 50   **Dot-to-Dot Decoding**

Review

daily almanac activities

mental math

- Count by 3's from 3 to 36.

- How many feet are in one yard? Ten yards? One hundred yards?

- Tony paid a dollar for an item that cost 78¢. How much money should he get back? What coins should he get back?   *22¢; 2 dimes, 2 pennies*

- Count by 5's from 2 to 42.   *2, 7, 12, 17, 22, 27, 32, 37, 42*

- Count by eighths from $\frac{1}{2}$ to $1\frac{1}{2}$.

problem solving

- Jimmy used twelve floor tiles to make a rectangle with a perimeter of 16 feet. Jamaal used twelve tiles to make a rectangle with a perimeter of 14 feet. Draw a sketch of both rectangles.

Materials Needed

- A copy of "Dot-to-Dot Decoding" (Master 22) for each student

Activity

In this activity students will make a design on a line grid. Pairs of numbers are given that name points on the grid. Students are to draw lines from point to point in the order listed to complete the design.

Guide students through the first few points so that they first move to the right and then up as they graph the points.

Extension: Some students may want to number grid paper, create their own designs, and write a dot-to-dot code for other students to decode.

MASTER 22   **DOT-TO-DOT DECODING**

Exercise 1   Graph these points and draw segments to connect them in order.

1. (10, 5)	5. (10, 3)	9. (3, 3)	13. (2, 7)
2. (9, 7)	6. (5, 3)	10. (2, 3)	14. (4, 7)
3. (16, 4)	7. (4, 1)	11. (2, 5)	15. (5, 5)
4. (9, 1)	8. (2, 1)	12. (3, 5)	16. (10, 5)

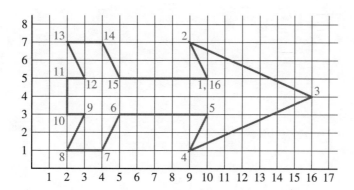

Exercise 2   Graph these points on a line grid. Then draw segments to connect the points in order.

1. (7, 2)	6. (4, 2)	11. (5, 9)
2. (9, 2)	7. (4, 3)	12. (5, 3)
3. (8, 1)	8. (5, 3)	13. (6, 3)
4. (2, 1)	9. (5, 4)	14. (7, 2)
5. (1, 2)	10. (2, 4)	

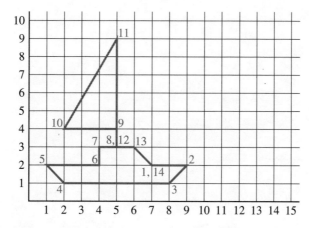

MASTER 1   TEMPERATURE LINE GRAPH

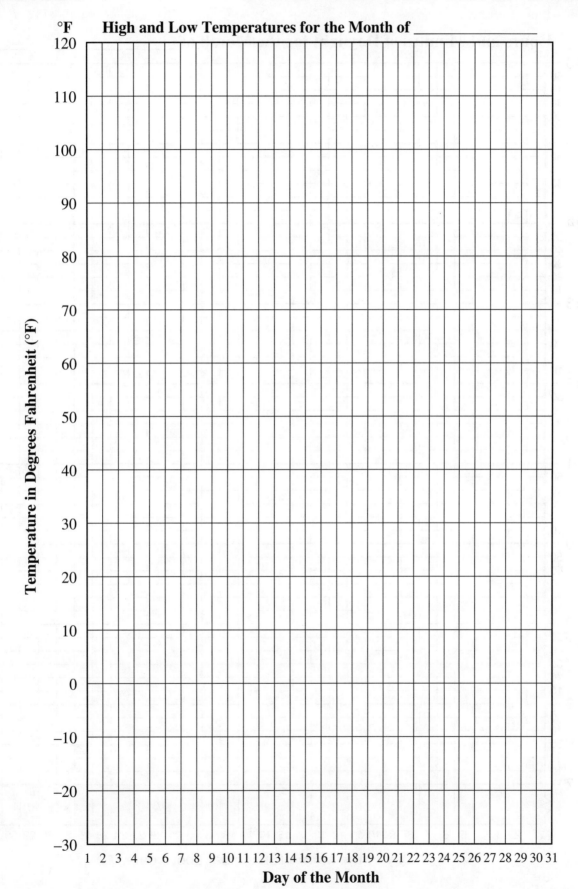

°F **High and Low Temperatures for the Month of** _____

Day of the Month

MASTER 2   # DAYLIGHT BAR GRAPH

Hours and Minutes of Daylight for the Month of _____

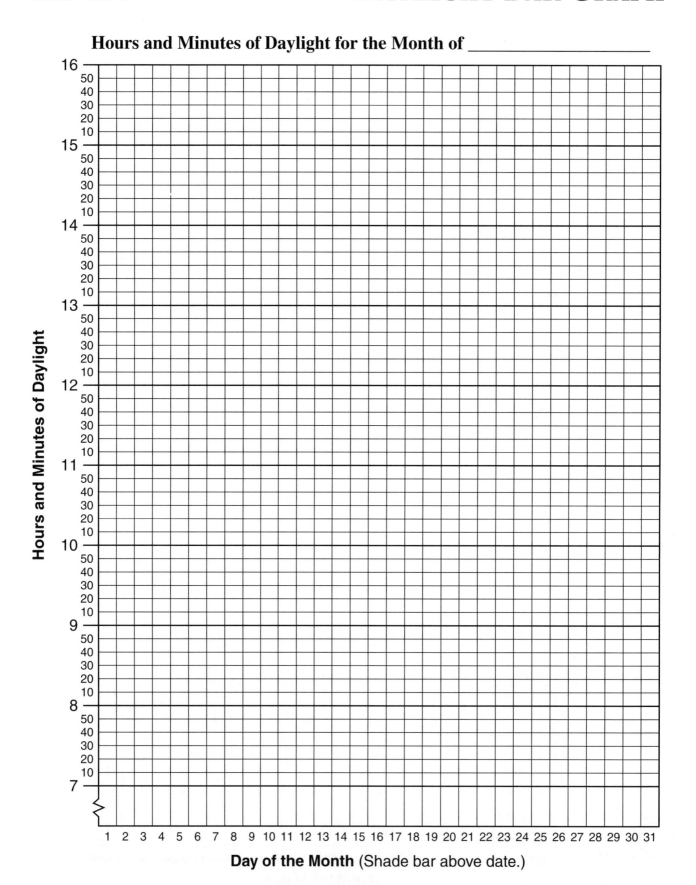

Day of the Month (Shade bar above date.)

Master 3   One-Dollar Bill Play Money

TEN-DOLLAR BILL PLAY MONEY

HUNDRED-DOLLAR BILL PLAY MONEY

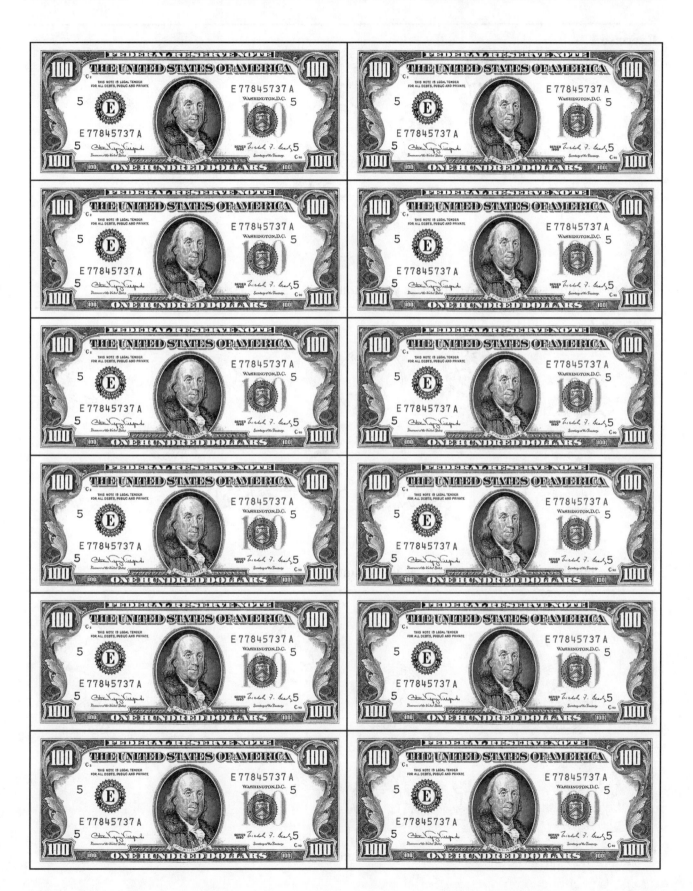

MASTER 6 — COUNTING COINS

Exercise 1

Write the numbers you say to yourself as you count.   Total Value: _____

Exercise 2

Write the numbers you say to yourself as you count.   Total Value: _____

Exercise 3

Write the numbers you say to yourself as you count.   Total Value: _____

_____ 20____

PAY TO THE
ORDER OF _____ $ [   ]

_____ DOLLARS

YOUR BANK, U.S.A.
Memo: _____   _____

_____ 20____

PAY TO THE
ORDER OF _____ $ [   ]

_____ DOLLARS

YOUR BANK, U.S.A.
Memo: _____   _____

_____ 20____

PAY TO THE
ORDER OF _____ $ [   ]

_____ DOLLARS

YOUR BANK, U.S.A.
Memo: _____   _____

UNITED STATES MAP

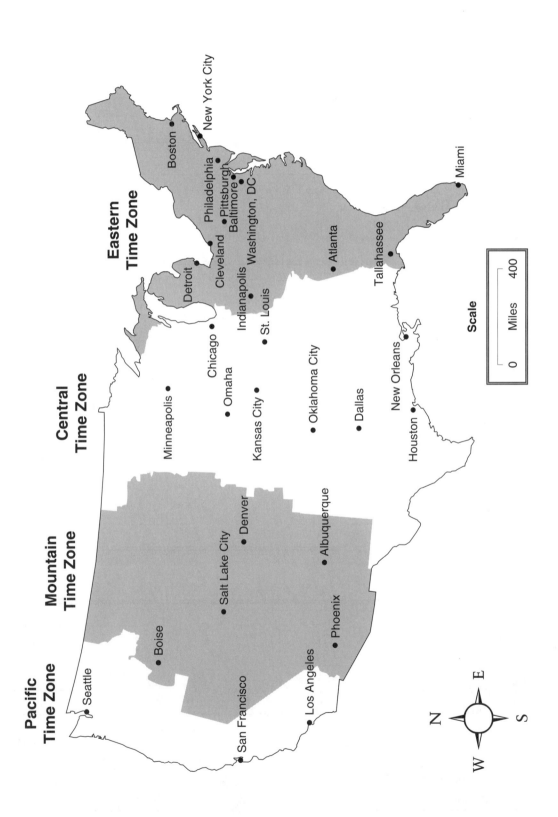

Scale

0   Miles   400

Eastern Time Zone

Central Time Zone

Mountain Time Zone

Pacific Time Zone

New York City
Boston
Miami
Philadelphia
Pittsburgh
Baltimore
Washington, DC
Cleveland
Atlanta
Tallahassee
Detroit
Indianapolis
St. Louis
Chicago
Omaha
Oklahoma City
New Orleans
Minneapolis
Kansas City
Dallas
Houston
Denver
Albuquerque
Salt Lake City
Boise
Phoenix
Seattle
San Francisco
Los Angeles

N
E
S
W

NEIGHBORHOOD MAP

Quincy

D

C   Monroe

Franklin   Knox   Hamilton   Gates

Madison

Jefferson

Lexington

E Adams

Adams

Franklin   Knox   Hamilton   Hale   Gates

Washington

A Hancock

Penn

B

Legend

School

A Alphie's house

B Brian's house

C Caleb's house

D Diana's house

E Eddie's house

MASTER 10 ESTIMATING FEET AND YARDS

Practice stepping one yard.

	heel to heel	
1 foot	1 foot	1 foot
	toe to toe	

|← ——————— one yard ——————— →|

How long is the classroom?

Estimate in yards: _____   In feet: _____

Measure in yards: _____   In feet: _____

How wide is the classroom?

Estimate in yards: _____   In feet: _____

Measure in yards: _____   In feet: _____

On this diagram, write the measured length and width of the room in feet.

length _____

| Classroom | width _____ |

Select a room at home to measure.

How long is the room?

Estimate in yards: _____   In feet: _____

Measure in yards: _____   In feet: _____

How wide is the room?

Estimate in yards: _____   In feet: _____

Measure in yards: _____   In feet: _____

Draw a diagram of the room you measured and write the measured length and width of the room in feet.

MAPS AND WRITTEN DIRECTIONS

First exercise:

Al told Gerard how to get to his house. He said, "Travel north on Highway 91 until you get to Kramer Road. Then turn right and travel east one mile to Evans Avenue. Turn right on Evans and go south one block to 362 Evans Avenue. We are on the left side of the street as you are heading south."

Sketch a map showing the route Gerard should travel to get to Al's house.

Second exercise:

Sherry gave Sarah a map to Sherry's house from the town where Sarah lives. Study the map and then write directions for Sarah describing how to get to Sherry's house.

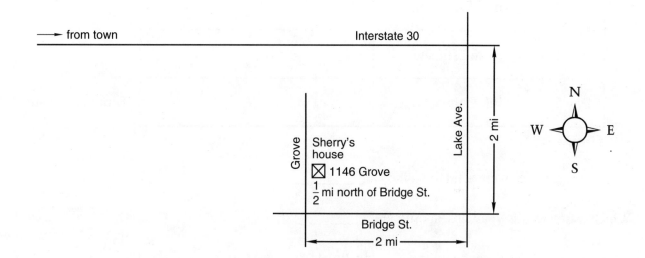

PENNY JAR ACTIVITY SHEET

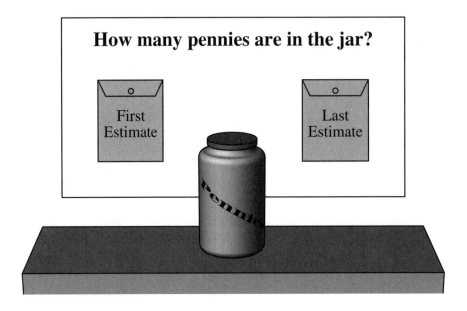

Record your estimates on this sheet. Once each day you will have a chance to improve your estimate.

Day 1	First Estimate		Turn in estimate
	Revised Estimate		
Day 2	Second Estimate		
Day 3	Third Estimate		
Day 4	Fourth Estimate		
Day 5	Fifth Estimate		Turn in estimate

How many pennies were actually in the jar? _____

Which estimate was your closest estimate? _____

Which activity helped you to improve your estimate the most? _____

DOUBLE YOUR MONEY TABLE

	John's Pay		James' Pay	
	Day's Pay	Total Pay	Day's Pay	Total Pay
Day 1	$1	$1	1¢	1¢
Day 2	$1	$2	2¢	3¢
Day 3	$1	$3	4¢	7¢
Day 4				
Day 5				
Day 6				
Day 7				
Day 8				
Day 9				
Day 10				
Day 11				
Day 12				

1. How much had each boy earned after 6 days?

_____

2. After which day were the boys' totals about the same?

_____

3. How much was each boy paid?

_____

4. What pattern can you find in the last two columns of the chart?

_____

Name_____

This diagram shows part of Holly's family tree.

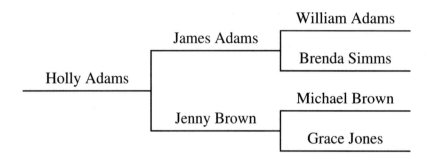

Who is Holly's grandfather on her mother's side? _____

What is Holly's father's mother's maiden name? _____

This diagram shows the games and winners in a table tennis tournament.

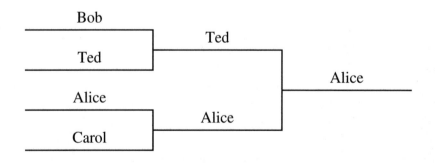

Who played Carol in the first match? _____

Who was the loser in the championship game? _____

Master 15 Measuring to the Nearest Eighth Inch

Find the length of each line segment.

1. ━━━━━━━━━━━━━━━━ The length is _____.

2. ━━━━━━━━━━━━━━━━━━━━━ The length is _____.

3. ━━━━━━━━━━━━━━━━━━━━━━━━━━━

   The length is _____.

Find the length and width of each rectangle.

4.

length _____

width _____

5.

length _____

width _____

6. How long is this paper? _____

   How wide is this paper? _____

Find the length of each object.

7. How long is your pencil? _____

8. How long is your little finger? _____

9. How long is your shoe? _____

10. Find an object to measure. Name the object and write its length.

    _____

DIVIDING MONEY IN HALF

	Amount	Even or Odd	Half of Amount
1.	$356		
2.	$365		
3.	$432		
4.	$423		
5.		even	
6.		odd	

Divide the amount of money in half. Put half of the money in each box.

Name_____   Name_____

MASTER 17

CALCULATOR ACTIVITY RECORDING SHEET

Number Entered	Even or Odd	Half of Number
37,254	even	18,627
1.		
2.		
3.		
4.		
5.		
6.		
7.		
8.		

Look for a pattern in this table. On the lines below, describe any pattern that you see.

Half of an even number _____

_____

Half of an odd number _____

_____

Read this story; then answer the questions.

Mark entered a number into a calculator and then divided by two. The calculator's display showed 1324.5.

a. Was the original number Mark entered even or odd? _____

b. How could you find the number Mark entered? _____

_____

c. Which number is larger, 1324.5 or $1324\frac{1}{2}$? _____

Name_____   Name_____

MASTER 18

LINES OF SYMMETRY ACTIVITY SHEET

Draw one line of symmetry for each figure:

1.  2. 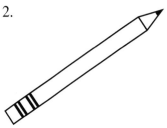 3.

Draw two lines of symmetry for each figure:

4. 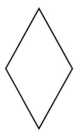 5. 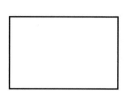 6.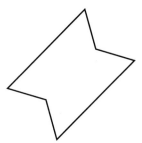

Draw one, two, or more lines of symmetry for each figure.
One figure has no lines of symmetry.

    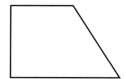

Describe what a line of symmetry is. Then draw a figure on the back of this paper that has a line of symmetry.

_____

_____

_____

QUARTER-INCH GRID

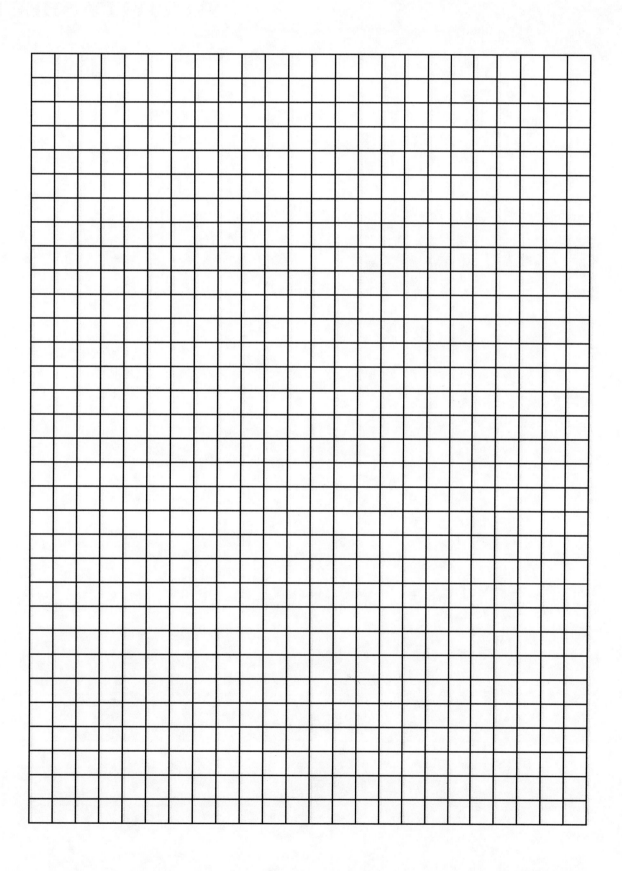

SQUARE-INCH GRID

PERIMETER AND AREA
OF RECTANGLES

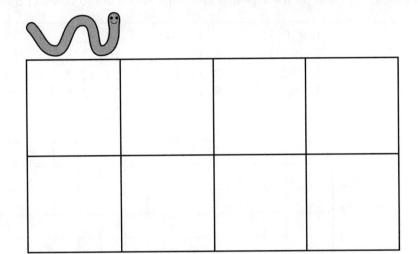

This is a 4-inch by 2-inch rectangle. It is 4 inches long and 2 inches wide. Its perimeter is 12 inches. Its area is 8 square inches.

Draw the four rectangles named in this chart on 1-inch grid paper. On the chart write the length, width, perimeter, and area of each rectangle.

	Rectangle	Length	Width	Perimeter	Area
1.	4 inch by 3 inch				
2.	6 inch by 2 inch				
3.	3 inch by 3 inch				
4.	8 inch by 1 inch				

DOT-TO-DOT DECODING

Exercise 1   Graph these points and draw segments to connect them in order.

1. (10, 5)	5. (10, 3)	9. (3, 3)	13. (2, 7)
2. (9, 7)	6. (5, 3)	10. (2, 3)	14. (4, 7)
3. (16, 4)	7. (4, 1)	11. (2, 5)	15. (5, 5)
4. (9, 1)	8. (2, 1)	12. (3, 5)	16. (10, 5)

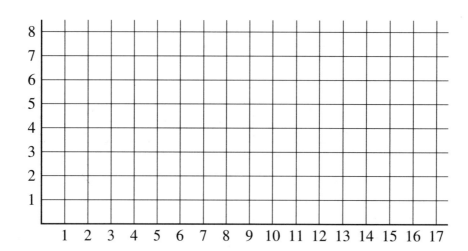

Exercise 2   Graph these points on a line grid. Then draw segments to connect the points in order.

1. (7, 2)	6. (4, 2)	11. (5, 9)
2. (9, 2)	7. (4, 3)	12. (5, 3)
3. (8, 1)	8. (5, 3)	13. (6, 3)
4. (2, 1)	9. (5, 4)	14. (7, 2)
5. (1, 2)	10. (2, 4)	

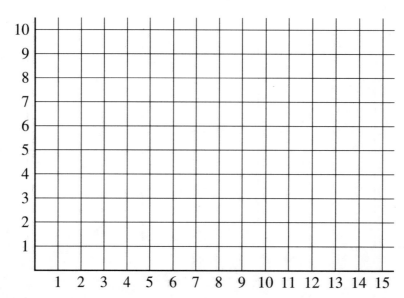